Learning Disabilities

Betty B. Osman

Learning Disabilities

A Family Affair

Random House New York

Library of Congress Cataloging in Publication Data

Osman, Betty B
Learning disabilities.

Bibliography: p.
Includes index.
1. Learning disabilities. I. Title.
LC4704.083   371.9   78–11509
ISBN 0–394–42127–2

MANUFACTURED IN THE UNITED STATES OF AMERICA

9 8 7 6 5 4 3

To all the children I have known
who have struggled to learn.
They have taught me the true meaning
of courage and perseverance.

A Note from the Author

I wrote this book primarily for parents who are concerned about their children and their children's learning. The priority placed on education today has made parents more aware than ever of their children's development and their progress in school. Yet too often, a mother's or father's expressed concerns are taken lightly by professionals or dismissed as the "anxious parent" syndrome. But parents, after all, are their children's first teachers, and their intuitions *are* to be trusted. Parents know their child and know what they see. It is the responsibility of educators to listen to parents and to provide them with the support and know-how to help their children survive in school and thrive at home. At the same time, it is the responsibility of parents to learn enough to know if they're getting good help.

From the moment a parent becomes aware of his or her child's possible learning difference or "developmental lag," another dimension is added to the family system. While a youngster's problems may in reality be centered in school, they quickly become a family affair, with widespread repercussions. All family members must make many practical adjustments—and even more emotional ones—that reflect the goals and values of the family as a group, as well as the needs of its individual members.

This book tries to help both parents and professionals recognize where children may be having difficulty and suggest ways to make their lives easier at home and at school. When children are content, their parents reap the rewards. It is on the premise that with information and insight come understanding, acceptance, and the ability to help one's children that this book is offered.

In writing this book, I had the support of both family and colleagues, for which I am deeply grateful. My husband, Al, encouraged me to tell this story, often at the sacrifice of time spent with him and our family. To him and to our children, I owe a debt of gratitude that cannot be measured.

This book could not have been written without my close friend and colleague, Henriette Blinder, who gave so generously of her time, her expertise, and her encouragement. I am more appreciative of her ideas, her criticism, and her help than can possibly be expressed. I give thanks to Joan Scobey, Harriet Blum, Kenny De Santis, and my sister, Carol Stern, for their assistance; to my graduate students for their enthusiasm and support; and to all the families with whom I have worked for providing me with the stories and the material for this book.

Contents

A Note from the Author   *vii*

1. Early Signs and Symptoms   *3*
2. It's a Family Affair   *26*
3. Life at Home   *41*
4. The Social Connection   *61*
5. Life at School   *84*
6. The Homework Question   *107*
7. Community Resources   *122*
8. What about the Future?   *140*

Notes   *156*
Bibliography   *159*
Appendices   *167*

Index   *214*

Learning Disabilities

Chapter 1

Early Signs and Symptoms

Though six months old, Jimmy rarely sleeps through the night and seems more restless and active than his sister did at that age. Betsy doesn't like kindergarten and can't seem to remember the names of her teacher or her classmates. Billy is four and hasn't learned color names or to count past five. Jeremy's first-grade teacher complains that he never sits still to listen to a story. Michael, eleven years old, never reads for pleasure, and Sarah is barely passing science and social studies in high school. Are these children of normal ability merely "slow" or "immature," or are they showing symptoms of a learning disability?

As parents, how do we handle Richard when his younger sister does better in school than he? And what about the family's questions as to why Jennifer doesn't read yet? These and many more questions might occur to you as your children grow and develop. Frequently, parents don't know whom to ask, and more important, they lack conviction and confidence in their own judgment, particularly when it comes to their young children's development and learning.

We hear so much these days about the importance of early diagnosis and treatment of learning disabilities, and yet Billy's nursery school teacher suggests that his parents "wait and see" when she mentions his "immaturity" and his "poor memory." And you might receive a similar "wait and see" from your family physician: "There's nothing physically wrong with Billy, and after all, he is only four. Wait and see."

As Billy's parents, though, you are not so sure. You may have many more questions but feel foolish asking them. You remember that Billy seemed rather cranky as an infant, he didn't babble as much or as early as his sisters, and he began to speak much later and with less clarity. And he never seemed able to remember that his favorite sneakers were red. Is there something wrong? On the other hand, maybe he's just like his uncle, a bit absent-minded and not too good with words. So you are reassured for a while. After all, he has learned to tie his shoelaces even earlier than Johnny next door, and he's had many fewer temper tantrums of late.

However, in the fall, Billy's kindergarten teacher notes that he is easily distracted and has trouble relating an event. "He can't seem to think of the right word, and he gets frustrated when his classmates don't wait for him to speak his mind." Then the question arises again. Is Billy simply "immature," or does he have a learning disability? What should you do?

"Learning disability" has become a familiar term for parents only in the past decade, but children with learning problems have been with us for centuries. Some very eminent people have found learning difficult: Thomas Edison, Albert Einstein, Winston Churchill, and Nelson Rockefeller, to name just a few. (There must have been some women, too, but their names are not as familiar.) How the children were labeled and treated, however, depended on the environment in which they lived and upon who pronounced the diagnosis.

To some extent, this is still true. Maybe you remember the class clown in your eighth-grade class. He was also, incidentally, the poorest reader in the class but you never made the connection. Looking back on it, perhaps he had learning disabilities. Teachers might have called him lazy, lacking in intelligence, unmotivated, emotionally troubled, dyslexic, brain injured, neurologically impaired, or perceptually handicapped, while a classmate who happened to be passing judgment might have said that he was just plain *dumb*. Sometimes, when learning is hard and a child feels unsuccessful and stupid, he'll do anything for attention and peer acceptance. As this boy might have expressed it many years later, "I wasn't such a good athlete. I had to do something to get friends."

Chances are that even today, an anxious parent, a frustrated classroom teacher, a psychologist, a neurologist, or a concerned grandparent will probably tend to view the same child quite differently. Each will see the child through the eyes of his or her own experience. Many parents know this all too well, having sought opinions and advice from many along the diagnostic trail.

⚡ But what is a learning disability? There has been much debate and concern about an appropriate definition. By and large, it is defined by exclusion—that is, by what it is *not.* The definition developed by the U.S. Department of Health, Education and Welfare is perhaps the most frequently used, although almost everyone agrees that it is imprecise and in need of revision. In essence, H.E.W. defines learning disabilities (LD) as disorders in the understanding or processing of language, including difficulties in listening, thinking, talking, reading, or math. However, these problems are not considered to be learning disabilities if they are primarily due to visual, aural, or motor handicaps, to mental retardation, to emotional disturbance, or to environmental disadvantage.*

One of the most glaring weaknesses in the H.E.W. concept, apart from its vagueness and definition in terms of what it isn't, is the very use of the term "learning disabilities." Although better than medical terms signifying brain injury or damage, the label "disabilities" is regrettable because it is both imprecise and not informative. It does not tell us in what areas the child is having difficulty, nor how we can help him. Few children look exactly alike, and very few children learn in exactly the same way or at the same chronological age. We all have areas of strength and weakness, which are reflected in our ability to learn and process information. In the final analysis, it's our abilities—things that we *can* do—that determine our success in accomplishing a task. Today, in our zeal for our children's academic success, we often focus too much on what they cannot do. It might be more productive to pay attention to those areas in which they *are* ready to learn!

*See Appendix for full text.

Recently professionals have begun to accept the idea that certain children can indeed learn, though somewhat differently from, and perhaps more slowly than, their peers. In referring to a child with a *learning difference*, we are describing a child with a discrepancy or lag between his overall intelligence and his apparent ability to learn in one or more areas. A youngster may not be able to express his thoughts easily, but he might be the class whiz at puzzles. Another child excels in math but cannot read, and he has trouble with sports.* Everyone has his own set of talents and areas of clumsiness, but when those areas affect a child's learning in school, we call it a learning difference.

Just as one swallow doesn't make a summer, no single pattern of behavior typifies a child for whom learning is difficult. In fact, there is no easily identifiable group of youngsters with learning differences. If we speak of a group at all, we have to be aware of the lack of anything in common among its members, with the possible exception of the discrepancy or lag mentioned earlier, and perhaps the effect of such a problem on the child and his family. Although the focus of a learning difference is usually in school or in a learning situation, its consequences are rarely confined to a youngster's difficulties in building with blocks, speaking, reading, spelling, or doing arithmetic problems. Many areas of a child's life are affected, including his role in the family, his relationship with friends, his prowess on the ball field, and surely his self-image and confidence in his ability to handle daily situations.

The diversity of children with so-called learning differences makes it hard for parents and teachers to recognize them. No two children look, learn, or behave in a like manner. For the sake of convenience, however, we can look at three general areas that encompass some of the symptoms of what might be a learning

---

*When the primary problem is reading, the child may be said to be dyslexic. Though dyslexia literally means nothing more than "a disturbance of the ability to read," it has become a catch-all word describing anything from a mild reading problem to a severe handicap. I try not to use the term for this very reason.

difference—remembering that all can simply be indicative of immaturity. These are

⊀ 1. language and concept development.
2. perceptual skills.
3. behavioral manifestations.

Of course, few if any children fit neatly into any one group. Looking at these categories is like reading a Chinese menu, where you take one from column A and one from column B. For the moment, though, let's look at some of the signs and symptoms from each group that you might see in your young child.

Language problems are an early indicator of a "child at risk" (another one of those professional terms you might hear from your doctor). When language is significantly delayed or immature for a prolonged time, it may signify that the child is having difficulty understanding, processing, or expressing verbal material. In an older child, this is sometimes referred to as a "specific language disability."

Children with language problems frequently seem less mature than their peers. They may not comprehend much of what is said to them and may even appear deaf to their worried parents. Many a parent has thought his or her child might be retarded because the child always responded "What?" when told to do something. Other children who hear and understand adequately may have trouble learning names of colors, teachers, and even familiar toys. In trying to tell me how the popcorn burned at nursery school, Peter said, "When my . . . you know, the lady at school [teacher] put the . . . thing [pot] on the . . . that thing you cook on [stove] the . . . corn pop got . . . black."

For children who have difficulty with language, processing and expressing their ideas are often hard. Prepositions are frequently mixed up, and ideas sometimes get turned around. Jill, a seven-year-old, used to say, "Mommy, I want to sit with you in the *back* seat when you drive," and "I'm hot. I want my sweater *on.*" Jeff, at twelve, couldn't pronounce the word "magnification." It kept coming out "magnicifation," no matter how hard he tried to say it correctly. Another teenager I treated was bewildered when he read that beavers build their homes "near a bank." He thought a bank was where his money went after Christmas. Such difficulties with language may affect a young child's speaking, and later, the reading, spelling, and written expression required in school.

Of course, inadequate language development might not signify a learning difference at all. It might mean many other things, ranging from retardation to emotional problems. Often even an experienced clinician cannot determine whether a particular behavior in a preschooler can be attributed to immaturity, a learning difference, or an emotional problem. In most instances, one should not be concerned with *why* a very young child acts as he does, unless the symptoms are severe and incapacitating. Worrying about causes often makes teachers, pediatricians, and parents reluctant to acknowledge a child's immaturity or learning difference, since they fear the ramifications of labeling. A fair amount of publicity in the past few years has centered on handicapped children, and surely no one wants to categorize or pigeonhole a three- or four-year-old as having a "learning disability" or any other problem that might later show up as a stain on his record at school. And parents and teachers usually *can* do much to help a young child catch up with himself in areas of development in which he lags behind—without formal diagnosis, labels, or stigmas.

The answer to the broader question of "Does my child have or does he not have a problem that will persist in the future?" is not always predictable and hardly seems an issue of immediate relevance. Rather, as his parent, you should focus on where he is in terms of his development. Careful observation of his behavior will make this clearer to you. You can and should acknowledge that he seems immature in some areas and do what you can to assist him. If a child's concepts or use of language don't seem up to par, for example, you may be able to help him on your own. Reading and talking to young children build an understanding of words and the concept that words are used to communicate ideas. And when you encourage your child to ask questions and express his thoughts, you are building a sense of competence as well as verbal fluency.

Two children with early indications of language difficulties come to mind. One was Jeremy, the youngest of five children. His language problems were reflected in the way he pronounced words and how he expressed his ideas. He was not quite five when I first saw him, but he had attended a day-care center for two years. He was an independent little boy, very advanced in manipulating objects with his hands. He dressed himself, could write his name, could copy geometric shapes, and could do puzzles with ease. Jeremy's mother told me that he had started to speak at approximately two years of age, but his speech remained indistinct and rather garbled. He was hard to understand, with his babyish articulation and misuse of words. He said "big" when he meant "little" and spoke of "early" whenever he meant "late." He also had difficulty naming objects, although his concepts seemed adequate for his age. He said once that windowpanes were made of "ice." Sometimes it seemed to require too much effort for Jeremy to try to express his thoughts verbally. At such moments he'd say, "Oh, nebber mind." Perhaps because of the difficulties he had communicating with the other children in the day-care center, he seemed immature socially, too. The children referred to him as "baby," which invariably brought tears and howls of frustration from Jeremy.

Jeremy's mother wondered if perhaps he "didn't have to speak" because of his position in the family. His older brothers and sisters gave him what he wanted, but at the same time never gave him a chance to talk. His mother realized Jeremy's need to describe his activities and thoughts and for his siblings to give him that chance at his own pace. I advised the family not to wait for Jeremy to struggle to find a word, but rather to supply it, thereby making his conversation more natural, fluent, and surely more useful to him. I also recommended that Jeremy remain for an additional year at the day-care center prior to kindergarten, and suggested that his teacher place emphasis on language development and social learning.

Danny, another four-year-old, had early symptoms of problems with language that were very different from Jeremy's. He came to see me after his mother had a conference with his nursery school teacher, a young, astute woman who reported that Danny was having trouble following directions. "He can't hold on to what you tell him. He echoes what is said to him, but he doesn't seem able to act on it. It seems as if I can't teach him by talking. He gets into trouble in school because he always does what his eyes see."

His parents described Danny, the younger of two boys in his family, as a "loving and lovable child, fun to be with most of the time," but they, too, had noticed certain things which puzzled them. His mother remembered that Danny started talking much later than his brother, Robert, but she felt that she had less time to spend with Danny and "perhaps he was watching too much TV." Both parents felt that perhaps they didn't spend enough time with Danny "doing constructive things." They agreed that Danny did not express himself well, although his speech was clear and his vocabulary was appropriate. He often seemed to "lose his train of thought while talking." Either his mother or his father had also observed:

- "Sometimes he ignores you or doesn't seem to hear. Maybe he's just being obstinate."

- "He has a tendency to say 'chickendary' for 'dictionary.' " His mother said she thought this was cute and she didn't try to correct Danny. She admitted babying him.

- "He sometimes tunes you out."

- "He hates loud noises and puts his hands over his ears when he hears a fire engine or the vacuum cleaner."

Jeremy's and Danny's stories are typical, not only because of some of the early signs and symptoms of a language difficulty, but also because of their parents' responses to those signs. I don't know what happened to Jeremy or Danny, but without intervention it is predictable that they would have had difficulty in school.

On the one hand, some parents tend to assume the responsibility for their children's every failure, and certainly for their learning problems. ("I must have done something wrong.") At the same time, they try to make excuses for them. ("Maybe he's been watching too much TV.") We tend to look for someone or something to blame for our children's problems and feel better if we can identify the source of the trouble, even if it's ourselves. In most cases, though, a youngster's learning differences are no one's fault, and we are usually unable to pinpoint the precise cause. The sources of difficulty may be myriad. It's usually a case of double jeopardy at least, with a cluster of symptoms present.

In contrast to children like Jeremy and Danny, who have trouble expressing themselves, are those talkative, highly verbal children whom everyone expects to be star performers. Their sophistication with words might mask learning differences involving *perception*—that is, how they understand and process information coming in through their senses. We see with our eyes, but we understand what we see with our brains. We are all familiar with the sight of parallel railroad tracks that appear to meet in the distance. No one would venture to board a train if our brains didn't assure us that our eyes were playing tricks on us; those rails really don't come together. It's just perspective, an optical illusion. If we were not able to perceive what we hear, see, taste, smell, and touch, and to learn from our perceptions, each experience would be a first, and we'd be hard put to get through a day's activities intact.

A child's first point of reference in the world around him is his own body. He learns up, down, big, tall, and front and back in terms of himself. We've all seen babies who back away from a toy they are trying to reach when they first learn to crawl. They have misperceived the direction in which they should move. It is also hard for a toddler to catch a ball because his hands and eyes don't coordinate and he can't judge precisely where the ball is in relation to him.

Some young children seem to trip over their own feet more than others, while others spill their milk too often and fall off chairs. This may be a sign of poor judgment in space. While such difficulties will not necessarily affect reading skills, they may lead to problems with math and geometry, in particular, as well as with one's performance as an athlete. It can be a long struggle. Barry, who is nine, has problems judging space and direction. His mother told me that with much practice and effort, Barry finally learned to hit the ball, "but then where on earth are the bases? He simply can't find them."

The old adage about "Which do we see, the doughnut or the hole?" may be an apt description of how some youngsters with problems see things. They have trouble noticing the bird on the grass or their teddy bear on the shelf. (Parents say, "He can't find something even if it's right in front of his nose.") The print on a page may confuse a child; words may tend to "move" when he begins to read or may "look different" from sentence to sentence. Kenny, age eleven, used to say that the pages "glared" and the words "jumped."

Even if seen and perceived accurately, a word that some children know on one page is unrecognizable a moment later. They have trouble remembering what they see. Later, in school, their misspelling of common words reflects this problem. "Uv [of]," "sed," and "cum" are good diagnostic tests, indicative of a poor visual memory for words in an older child. Roger, a bright twelve-year-old, could hear the way words should be spelled, but he could not see in his mind how they should look. After spending a weekend on a farm in Long Island, he wrote the following:

> I whent to Longe Ilind and got to rid on a bot and fede hourses and shas rabits. it was vere fun.

We can decipher what Roger meant, but he'll never win any spelling bees. He also has to cope with his teacher's reaction to his "carelessness"—and to the low grade she'll probably give him.

Many children who perceive visual stimuli accurately and whose hearing is within the normal range on a hearing test cannot make sense out of what they hear. Ronny, in third grade, heard a car honk outside. He looked puzzled and asked, "What was that, a firecracker?" Most of us wouldn't have to hesitate a moment before recognizing that sound and moving out of the car's path. With his difficulties, what would Ronny do? Other children have such acute hearing that they are distracted from the job at hand by the sound of a leaf rustling.

Some youngsters can understand what they hear but find it hard to listen attentively, perhaps reacting only to short units of language. They miss much of what is said to them because they cannot process it fast enough. (It's like a tourist trying to understand a foreign language, or a moviegoer seeing a foreign film. Though a few words or phrases might be "heard," most cannot be understood amid the barrage of unintelligible sounds.) For instance, you might ask your son to "go upstairs, get dressed, and bring down a sweater." He may only have heard the phrase "go upstairs," and he'll return still in his pajamas and empty-handed. He is not being deliberately disobedient; he simply cannot listen well enough. Incidentally, this is a skill that can develop with age and some careful handling by adults. Before accusing your children of being deaf, you might try speaking more slowly and giving them fewer directions at the same time.

Related to a child's ability to listen attentively are background noises and other distractions. So many children complain that they can't concentrate in class because "it's so noisy" and "the other kids bother me." Adults who have tried to hold a serious conversation at a nightclub or a large party can probably sympathize. We may be distracted by the music, the noise of dropped dishes, and the conversations of people nearby.

Some youngsters hear speech sounds imprecisely, so the many words that sound alike are confused. Carrie thought her father said "Your goat is dead," when in reality he had shouted "You go to bed!" Only Carrie's horrified expression told her father he had been misunderstood.

Most young children associate some words incorrectly at one time or another, as Meg, at age three, did when she begged me to take her swimming in the "noise." After a great deal of frustration caused by my inability to understand her, I finally realized that Meg was referring to Long Island Sound, a body of water nearby. Another child assured me he had seen the Monsters play football at Shea Stadium the previous night. Of course, he was referring to the Giants.

In order to be able to retell a story or the essence of a TV show, we have to recall it in sequence. Ordering sounds also presents problems for some children, who may continue to pronounce "aminal," "pisgetti," and "hopsital" long after this is usually outgrown. Some common effects of problems with putting things in their correct order are difficulties in learning to tell time, in naming the days of the week and months in order, and in knowing which letters and numbers precede others in the alphabet or in counting.

When the child in nursery school or kindergarten avoids such table activities as drawing, coloring, and cutting, it may signify that he is having trouble working with his hands. This problem may show up again when he can't learn to tie his shoes or to write letters in school. I've received many referrals from observant teachers who recognize that an older child who can participate actively in class discussions should not become immobilized when he has to put anything on paper. I recall Beverly, at eleven, who computed complex fractions in her head, but who couldn't solve the same problems on paper. And though Gene, an eighth grader, gave me an insightful oral review of *The Chariot of the Gods,* he couldn't begin to put his thoughts in writing coherently. He had to ask how to spell each and every word, and it was an effort for him to write. When I couldn't decipher his report (which is reprinted here), I asked him to read it to me, but even he couldn't make sense out of it. He said, "Wow! What I think and what I write are two different things."

Some children perceive well what they see, hear, and feel, but become confused when they have to combine the information that comes to them through separate senses. As parents, we're often puzzled by a child who can say the alphabet and recognize an A when he sees one, but can't remember how to write it. Martha Denckla, a neurologist, calls this the George Washington Bridge syndrome. "Everything's fine in New York and all is well in New Jersey, but it's the George Washington Bridge connection that's awry."

> the Chariots of the Gods
>
> This book Theroy is people once romaned the theroy avaced than will be 100yrs from now. They bought up alost of different thing's you argu with like the pymanals each block weigh a minum of 2 tons and they are 20ft tall as the whole thing there so many of them mathnaticly over the years and no. of slaves They couldnit do this and the archrce of them was fantic.

While some children have learning differences that center on either language or perception, a third group display early signs and symptoms in their general *behavior*. Parents have reported that, even as infants, their children were "moody," "active," "restless," "always running," "exhausting but never exhausted," "stubborn," "fearful," and "lacking in caution and good sense." Sometimes teachers claim that a student has trouble getting along with his classmates. He tends to tease them and to be naive or gullible. He seems generally immature. He may be the class clown or scapegoat. The same child may tell you that he dislikes recess "'cause there's nothing to do outside and the kids are mean." In the neighborhood, these children often seek the younger children with whom to play, but any friendships they form are rarely longstanding or smooth.

Another frequently heard complaint from parents is a youngster's fear of change or his reluctance to try anything new. One child became hysterical when his father deviated from his usual route to his office. This threatened the child, who had depended on a familiar pattern. With little confidence and security in their own perceptions of the world, it is no wonder that children only rely on and trust the familiar, the tried and true.

Psychologists often think of these social maladjustments as "emotional," to differentiate them from "learning" problems, but they are really part of the same general difficulties. A child's world is unsteady in every aspect when learning is hard!

Seth, the oldest child in his family, was born while his father, a pediatrician, was in the Navy and away much of the time. His mother felt alone in her new home away from relatives and friends, particularly since Seth was not an easy baby from the beginning. He seemed high-strung, demanding, and very active. He learned to walk and talk at appropriate ages, though, and eventually the family returned to their home state, where Seth started school.

Seth's progress in school was slow, and he continued to be a challenge to his parents. When he was in second grade, his father and mother realized that much of the family tension stemmed from Seth. He was cranky, had increasingly frequent temper tantrums, and was mean and nasty to his sisters. At school, his teacher was frustrated, too. She told his parents that though Seth seemed bright, he certainly was not learning what she was trying to teach. He was so fidgety and disruptive in class that the other children were beginning to reject him.

It seemed to Seth's parents that their son had emotional problems and that perhaps this was the reason for his poor work in school. His father asked a colleague for advice about whom to consult to find out how to help Seth—and the family.

My evaluation revealed that Seth was intelligent. (He tested in the superior range on WISC-R, a standardized IQ test.) His problems were not just emotional ones, though. Seth was reading at a mid-first-grade level, approximately one year below the level expected for his actual grade in school, but far below the reading ability of most of his classmates. He could not recall words at sight (reflecting poor visual memory), and he had to sound out almost every word on a page. This made reading laborious and frustrating for him. No wonder he hated to read! Seth also had problems with writing. His manuscript resembled the uneven scratches of a lame chicken limping across a page, and it took Seth a long time to form even a shaky letter. The pencil was hard to control, and with his inability to visualize a word, spelling was hopeless. In contrast with his difficulties with reading and writing, Seth's fund of knowledge and his ability to speak in class were superior—when he could pay attention, that is. Usually he found himself thinking of other things until his teacher yelled at him. All in all, school was not a happy or rewarding place for Seth. Is it surprising that he was cranky and irritable?

A word about Seth's "emotional problems." He surely had a volatile temperament, and perhaps his family situation created some additional difficulties for him. Nevertheless, he did have a significant learning difference that undoubtedly contributed to his weak self-image and his frustration. When he was helped to learn to read and write, his disposition improved, along with his social relationships. His parents were relieved, too, and began to enjoy Seth's sparkly, if intense, personality.

We know some of the difficulties with which children with learning differences struggle, but *why* is learning so hard for them? Causation is even more complex than the symptoms, and it is difficult at times to determine just which combination of factors is relevant in making it hard for a child to progress. We may just have to treat what we see. This is sometimes difficult for parents and teachers to accept, but it's hard to be absolutely scientific when you're dealing with human behavior. There's no bacteria to immunize against, and you can't remove the problem like an inflamed appendix.

A rather irreverent story was told by an authority on learning disabilities who attended a three-day conference. Many of the prominent people in the field were there. According to the agenda, the first day was to be spent defining terms, such as "learning disabilities" and "dyslexia." The second day's topic was diagnosis of learning disabilities, and the third day was to deal with methods of treatment. "The first day," this gentleman reported, "we were unable to agree on a single definition or term. We fared no better with diagnosis on the second day, but that didn't keep us from arriving at appropriate modes of treatment on the third day."

People interested in children's learning have tried to identify *causes* of learning differences. It seems that the more comprehensive the study, the greater the number of related causes that might be found. One study at the Learning Center in Binghamton, New York, attempted to rate the causal factors in 154 children with learning problems. General immaturity was the most frequently considered reason, followed by emotional problems, poor socioeconomic background, and others. Usually the many factors that contribute to a learning difference interact and interrelate in the living, breathing child and cannot be singled out.

However, let's mention some of them that might combine to make learning difficult for so many children.

1. Intelligence. Learning differences occur in all segments of the population, from the gifted to the retarded, but professionals tend to speak of learning disabilities only for the children of average or above-average ability. Actually, this is not necessarily so. Children of all ranges of intelligence can have learning problems.

Youngsters of superior ability who are just making it in school are showing evidence of underachievement and perhaps a learning difference. They should be doing better! It goes without saying that a retarded child will have difficulty learning, but we don't usually think of gaps in his development as being the primary cause of his lack of success in school or in life.

According to many researchers, the most that intelligence does is limit the amount of achievement or the rate at which a child might learn. It does *not* predict how well he will or will not learn. Motivation, the quality of teaching, and family goals, among other factors, play a determining role.

The way parents and teachers see a child relates to his ability, too. One well-known study[1] showed the effect of teachers' expectations on children's achievement in school. When supervisors told teachers that children in their classes were extremely capable and should accomplish a great deal during the year, the children achieved beyond anyone's expectations. However, when told that a class was "dull" according to intelligence tests and that not much could be expected, the youngsters accomplished little. This occurred despite the fact that the make-up of the two classes was similar. The implications for teaching, particularly in urban or economically deprived areas, are enormous. If we lower our expectations for students because of the environment from which they come, we may be encouraging failure through a self-fulfilling prophecy. Children need standards and expectations in order to fulfill their promise as learners.

2. *Sensory deficits.* Alluded to earlier in this chapter, these are deficiencies in the working of our eyes and ears, or with the central nervous system's connections from those organs. To hear music or see a sunrise, one's ears and eyes must be healthy. But some children with 20/20 vision and perfect hearing will misinterpret sensory impressions because of a central nervous system dysfunction. Their brains give them the wrong messages. In the 1960's, perceptual training programs were very much in vogue as a means of improving children's learning. The training consisted of remedial activities designed to correct a child's perception of basic sights and sounds without using academic materials.

In the height of the perceptual training era, I received a phone call one evening from a parent who wanted me to see his child for educational therapy. He asked no questions about my qualifications or my ability to work with his son except "Do you Frostig?" (He apparently had little knowledge of the use of these perceptual-training materials, but he had heard the name.)[2] There is less faith today that retraining sensory pathways will affect academic learning, although teaching young children to perceive their surroundings more adequately might help prepare them for school.

Just as each of us has his own style of learning, so, too, does the youngster for whom learning is difficult. One child will remember a word on a page by picturing it in his mind, while another will mentally hear the sounds to form a meaningful association. Eventually, most of us learn, albeit unconsciously, to live with and compensate for our weaker areas. We use marketing lists, date books, and memory hooks, such as mnemonic devices, in order to function in daily life. And if jigsaw puzzles are frustrating for us, we can avoid them. Just as we can provide children with glasses to help them compensate for inadequate visual acuity, so, too, should we look for appropriate ways to teach children to help them compensate for deficits.

3. *Activity level and attention span.* This refers to a child's ability to stay in his seat and concentrate. A child has to pay attention to the task at hand in order to learn. Much-discussed symptoms of learning differences include distractibility, lack of attention, and impulsivity. When youngsters can't concentrate on any one thing for more than a moment, it's not necessarily that they can't pay attention to what's going on around them. They may be noticing *everything* in sight—and all at the same time. Some children are unable to disregard the less important things in their environment. Everything captures their interest, although briefly. This has become known as the Strauss syndrome. Two early researchers in the field, Alfred Strauss and Laura Lehtinen, felt that distractibility and impulsivity were almost synonymous with learning disabilities.

The hyperactive child is usually easy to spot. He can sit for only a few minutes at a time and wiggles and fidgets even while sitting. I once saw a tiny tot not more than one and a half years old running barefoot a mile a minute through a department store, her exasperated father in tow. Her parents were trying in vain to buy her shoes. I smiled sympathetically, commenting, "She's really quite active, isn't she?" The little girl's mother retorted without hesitation: "Hyperkinetic, you mean!" She obviously knew whereof she spoke. While every hyperactive child does not necessarily have a learning disability, there is a high correlation between the two.

Teachers, parents, and friends of the family tend to use the term "hyperactive" quite freely these days to explain the cause of a youngster's inattention or distractibility. Actually, this term may be misleading. A child might be hyperactive or hyperkinetic (the latter signifies a neurologically caused inability to sit still), but then again, he might just be restless or "all boy." Hyperactivity may also reflect the judgment of the beholder more than the behavior of the child. Sometimes it is simply a question of "hyperactivity as compared with what?" Harry's mother complained that her son was hyperactive. To observers, though, Harry did not seem overly active; he was simply more energetic than his older sister had been.

Some children are perceived as hyperactive in school, particularly by teachers who have a need for order and tranquillity in their classrooms. They may not be tolerant of behavior that might be perfectly acceptable to other teachers. Charlie, who was disruptive in a structured classroom, had no trouble when he was moved to a more "open" and relaxed class. That teacher didn't mind if he stood up to work, and she expected him to move from one station to another in the classroom to complete assignments.

4. *Brain injury and minimal brain dysfunction (MBD)*. Some school-related problems may have their origin in prenatal, birth, or postnatal trauma. Prematurity, low birth weight, blood incompatibility, anoxia (a lack of oxygen supply to the brain either during or after birth), or a serious physical injury may significantly affect a child's ability to learn. In most cases, we can only speculate about the precise cause. There is no proof. Even an EEG (electroencephalogram), a recording of brain waves, is usually inconclusive. Also, many children with recognizable neurological impairment, such as cerebral palsy and seizure disorders, learn extremely well. The relationship between organic impairment and learning is far from clear.

Today, biochemical factors are also being researched as possible causes of learning disabilities. Current studies are investigating the chemical structure of foods and drugs and their effects on the human body. Although the results of research in this area only suggest a connection between food and learning problems at this time, some parents and professionals maintain that children's sensitivity to sugar and/or food additives contribute to their difficulties in school.[3]

5. *Genetic factors*. A family history of learning problems, including those of grandparents, aunts, and uncles, is sometimes a clue to a youngster's problems. I wish I had a nickel for every father of a child with learning differences who remembers having

been a poor speller in school. Just as artistic talent and athletic ability seem to run in families, so does the tendency to find reading or arithmetic difficult. There is also a sexual connection —at least five times as many boys are affected as girls, according to some of the more moderate figures.

6. *Immaturity or maturational lag.* Probably the most frequently heard reason for a child's learning difference, this is by far the most acceptable to parents. In most instances, it is also probably true! A youngster may just be developing more slowly than his peers *in some areas*. It's not the number of candles on a child's birthday cake, after all, that determines his readiness to learn, but rather his rate of development and level of maturity. If a child is physically small, is late to lose his baby teeth, and perhaps walks and talks somewhat later than his brother, we might well expect his learning to follow suit. But his problems are compounded if he is placed in school according to his age rather than his readiness to learn.

Parents and teachers respect individual differences among children only up to a point. No one worries if Johnny doesn't learn to swim at the same age as the boy next door or if he gets his permanent teeth a few months after everyone else on the block, but we *do* expect Johnny to learn to read, willy-nilly, at the age of six. There is little flexibility about requirements here.

Some researchers have suggested that frequently a child's apparent learning differences are the result of his being "overplaced" in school. Arnold Gesell and Louise Ames,[4] for example, recommend that the first course of treatment for a child with learning problems is either to retain him in a grade for another year or to place him in a lower grade. This is a complicated matter I'll discuss later, but it has been found that fewer reading problems exist in the early grades in Sweden, where children begin school at the age of seven.

7. *Emotional factors.* People have debated the significance of emotional factors in learning differences for years. Under what conditions do emotional problems cause learning difficulties? We all know many troubled children who are highly motivated to learn and very successful in school. Perhaps one of the most

important reasons for others' school failure lies in the key word fear—fear of trying and failing, fear of competing with an exceptional brother or sister, or even the fear of growing up and assuming responsibility for one's actions. Or an anxious, nervous child with a lot on his mind just might not be able to concentrate on the symbols in front of him. Robby, in third grade, told me he was "too sad and worried about [his lack of] friends to care much about schoolwork." His teacher agreed that his mind was usually anywhere but on the pages assigned.

Too much pressure to achieve might have a paradoxical effect. Larry, fourteen, said that his parents thought only intellectual pursuits mattered. His interest in and talent for sports earned no recognition at home, only jibes about his being a "jock." In his anger and sadness at not being accepted for himself, he tuned out at school until he failed most of his subjects.

Then, too, a learning difference itself is likely to cause an emotional problem for a child who has met failure at school. It would be an unusual youngster who could withstand frustration and failure at school every day and not respond emotionally. How could he possibly maintain his equanimity and good feeling about himself?

8. *Environmental factors.* These include malnutrition, a lack of language experience, and cultural deprivation. Children who are chronically malnourished cannot possibly perform well. We know how hard it is to perform our daily tasks when we are tired or not feeling up to par. When a large group of youngsters in an urban area were given a hot breakfast every day, their school achievement rose considerably. Their intelligence, as measured on an IQ test, did too.

Cultural deprivation is not confined to poverty areas. Just because a child is well dressed or lives in the suburbs, he is not necessarily immune to deprivation. Children who are left in the care of uneducated and perhaps uninterested household help may suffer from a lack of experience with word meanings as well as with ideas. Lisa, ten, tried hard not to care when she realized that her mother could not stay home from work when Lisa was on vacation from school. "At least I could watch TV all day," she said with a smile. We would agree that her day was quiet and relaxing, though in all probability this electronic "mother substitute" would not do much to augment Lisa's concepts or her vocabulary.

9. *Educational factors.* Inappropriate or inadequate teaching may also be a consideration in some children's learning problems, although this is obviously an unpopular idea with educators. Youngsters often seem to learn by osmosis, regardless of curriculum and teaching methods. But for a few children, the quality and consistency of teaching are crucial. Materials for cultural diversity are sadly lacking in most schools, and some children may have a hard time relating to the curriculum and concepts taught. If we think that the old Dick and Jane are misplaced in today's world, think how today's city child might respond to tales of farm life and whimsy! New materials in school must take this into account.

We expect teachers to know a great deal about a very challenging field. Yet until recently (January 1976 in New York State), many certified elementary teachers had never taken a course in the teaching of reading during their training. None was required! And even fewer teachers at any level have had either experience with learning differences or instruction in teaching the special children in their classes.

Teachers often overlook how a child learns or how he may be compensating for specific kinds of learning problems. I counseled one teenager who reported that even with a huge file documenting his inability to spell and write throughout his school career, his tenth-grade English teacher still gave him an F on a paper, with the following note: "Your spelling is careless and your handwriting, sloppy. This is unacceptable. Please rewrite." When Carlos discussed this with her, she told him that she had deliberately not read his old school records so as "not to become prejudiced" in her judgment of him.

Sometimes teachers may inadvertently present learning activities in such a way as to complicate learning for a few children with more than their share of problems. A "sight word" approach to reading, formerly called the "look and say" method by the last generation of teachers, may be an inappropriate choice for a young child who can't remember what a word looks like. One important note: some children might lack the prerequisite skills for the instruction or concepts offered at a particular time. It may well be the child who is out of step, not his teacher—but this too must be understood.

None of these causes of learning differences stands alone; at least several interact, affecting each child differently. No two children are alike; each responds in a different way to similar conditions, and in turn invites very different reactions from parents and teachers.

But as I mentioned before, it is not usually necessary to know the origins of the problem to help a child. Rather, professionals should momentarily forget their research projects and parents should try to ignore their own feelings of guilt so that they can become more aware of their child's difficulties and pain. A youngster with a learning difference needs a lot of understanding and help from supportive people, particularly from his family.

Chapter 2

It's a Family Affair

Chances are good that you're reading this book because a professional has told you that your child has a learning disability. Your memory of the fateful school conference at which you heard this news may be very dim. Perhaps you weren't even sure what Billy's teacher was talking about. He said something like "He's having difficulty learning to read . . . We might want to retain him in first grade next year." Since you probably felt as if you had been kicked hard in the solar plexus, the rest of the conference may remain a blur. You might even have forgotten about the vague worries you had about your child when he was a preschooler, but now that an educator had seen his problems, you had to confront them. You wanted to ask several questions but you were afraid you might burst into tears before you left the school. It was a painful moment and hardly what you had envisioned when Billy started school in September.

All too frequently, parents become aware of a youngster's learning problems only after he begins elementary school. You may have had an earlier suspicion of something not quite right, but no one really talked about it until his difficulties at school became obvious. Nursery school teachers and pediatricians tend to be reluctant to talk with parents about a young child's learning problems on the basis that in all probability he is merely immature and will do better next year. Why alarm his parents needlessly? Sometimes the child may have reached fourth or fifth grade before his parents are finally called to school to discuss his learning difference. As an extreme example, I recently saw a girl whose reading problems weren't noticed until she was in the eleventh grade. She'd been fooling most of the people most of the time, and she had probably survived in school by her wits. She was a bright young lady who absorbed a great deal of information by listening attentively. She participated actively in class discussions and even wrote book reports on books she had never read. It is rare, though, that difficulties are recognized that late. Parents and teachers probably ignored some of the earlier signs. Indications of this girl's problem—and the potential for remediation—were probably there long before her junior year in high school.

Parents have described their initial reactions to hearing about their children's learning differences. Sometimes the feeling is one of relief. Their suspicions are finally confirmed. But more often the response to the news is amazement, shock, disbelief, and especially anger—at the teacher, the school, and particularly the child. In retrospect, many parents realize that this first "professional diagnosis" has even made them look at their child differently. Suddenly the youngster appeared less mature, less competent, and surely, less successful. Some parents have even said that their children "looked different," resembling for the first time that black-sheep brother or other unsuccessful relative whom no one mentions any more.

Accepting the idea of a child's learning problems is an ongoing process and a painful learning experience for parents. It doesn't happen all at once during one conference at school or in a physician's office. Indeed, complete acceptance or understanding may not be possible at all! The feelings that emerge along the way are many and ever-changing, and they may be very different for each member of the family.

While feelings are quite varied and as individual as fingerprints, I have noticed that most parents go through similar emotional stages after being told of a child's learning difference. The feelings may even parallel those emotions experienced after a severe loss or the death of someone close. Maybe, in a sense, there is a loss—the loss of the "super-child" for whom parents might have hoped.

When a professional (physician, school psychologist, or teacher) expresses concern about your youngster's learning, you may respond with disbelief or denial. "He always seemed so bright" or "She must be wrong" may be your initial thoughts. You might shop around at this time for a professional who agrees with you. Then, later on, there is anger: "What does she know about my child?" or "It must be the way she's teaching him." At this time, parents may look with envy and even annoyance at other children who are more successful in school. "Why Billy?" or "Why is this happening to us?" are questions frequently asked. Typically, you might try to place the blame on your spouse, on the school, or even on Billy, for "not trying" or for being "lazy."

In time, as happens after a death, the anger gives way to feelings of resignation and finally acceptance. Now you might say, "Billy does have a problem. What should we do?" Although you might have stormed out of that first conference, angry and upset with the authority who confronted you with the news, you may now, weeks or months later, be ready to accept advice and offers of help. That is when effective treatment can begin. Too often, a psychologist or representative of the school explains the problem to parents, feels their anger, and decides that they are "difficult people, impossible to work with." Having thus dismissed the parents, these professionals have in effect closed the door to future contacts.

Parents should not be intimidated by a professional who becomes impatient or intolerant of their feelings. It may not be easy to do, but they should try to return to ask more questions and to clarify their feelings. If they continue to feel frustrated, they may want to request a conference with someone else in the school, perhaps the principal or psychologist. Parents also have the right to ask that a report from the school be sent to an outside professional for interpretation. I have been a back-up person for many parents who felt misunderstood by professionals.

Just as it is important for parents to recognize that understanding a child's learning difference is an ongoing process, professionals must be aware that parents may well not hear or understand the problem the first time it is explained. Their responses are all part of the natural process of working it through, and it is our responsibility, as professionals, to keep the lines of communication open so parents can come back when they are ready to hear and to be helped.

The director of a clinic for youngsters with learning disabilities told a professional audience that if his staff could not work successfully with parents, the clinic refused to treat the child. He had apparently forgotten that the parents had voluntarily sought the help from the clinic in the first place! Sometimes what comes across to professionals as hostility and antagonism is really only an expression of the frustration and anxiety many parents feel so keenly.

Parents' feelings about their children determine to a great extent the youngsters' attitudes toward both learning and themselves. Some of the loudest messages that children receive from their parents remain unspoken. Some children seem particularly tuned in to moods or feelings around them, to body language and facial expressions. They know when their parents are upset and conversely, when their parents can be depended upon for support and reassurance. In a study by Doreen Kronick,[1] learning-disabled children appeared particularly vulnerable to family problems and tension. They were acutely aware of their parents' disappointment and frustration with them. And since it is not easy to live in a family with a child who requires enormous doses of time and attention, sisters and brothers also feel the "vibes" and react accordingly. Children's learning differences are, indeed, a family affair! Whether or not a family discusses the problems openly or keeps them a secret, everyone in the family responds in some way to the child's difficulties.

Parents may feel guilty about their children's troubles with learning. A mother or father might think, *Maybe it's my fault. I should have taught him more,* or *It must have come from my side of the family.* One young mother recalled her disappointment in her child: "He was clumsy, he didn't talk, and he clung to me all the time. I felt that I had failed as a mother."

Sometimes there is resentment between the parents. One may feel that the cause of the child's dysfunction lies with the other, particularly if the spouse has also had difficulty in school. I've often heard something similar to the following: "He's just like his dad and his grandfather. Their sense of direction is terrible. They never could find their way home from next door." While these feelings may be a natural reaction to frustration, pointing an accusing finger really doesn't help. Your spouse may be feeling very guilty and doesn't need to be attacked. In fact, if he has had similar problems, he may become his child's best ally.

A child with a problem sometimes lowers a parent's self-esteem, which imposes an additional strain on a marriage. We know from studies that a child's imperfect physical or mental condition may threaten parents' feelings of competence and self-worth. Self-doubt tends to generate even more guilt, often accompanied by a feeling of helplessness. Frustration and helplessness become associated with anger, which is often unwittingly expressed toward the child. When we can't handle feelings and have no place to express them directly, anger is a common response.

When parents suffer from guilt or anger, they often find it hard to talk about their feelings. I had seen eight-year-old Bobby for six months before I realized that his father didn't know he was coming for help. (I almost always meet both parents before seeing a child, but this time was different.) Bobby's mother was unable to discuss his problem with anyone, even her husband. Bobby had been adopted in spite of some strong family opposition and his mother could not admit that something might be wrong with him. Perhaps some part of her, too, felt that the adoption was a mistake. Many months later, she phoned, relieved, to say that when her mother-in-law had noticed Bobby's difficulty with reading, she had told her everything. To her surprise, Bobby's grandmother understood and even expressed her willingness to help.

Some parents don't feel any guilt or anger about a youngster's problems. They just don't feel anything at all—or at least think they don't. They dismiss his learning problems as unimportant, if they acknowledge them at all. "So long as Jim is a good boy and gets along well with his friends on the ball field, we are satisfied." Sometimes this can actually work to a youngster's advantage. When he goes home after school, no one judges him by how well he can read. Since he is not constantly confronted with failure, home truly becomes a refuge and a haven. However, this may also mean that his difficulties are disregarded, and therefore untreated. Everyone takes the clue from his parents' denial; even the school may be afraid to rock the boat by discussing his problems.

Miles was in fifth grade before his parents brought him for remedial help, and then only because the school had insisted. In our initial meeting, his parents said they weren't even sure that Miles had a problem worthy of my attention, but the school apparently felt strongly that he did. Miles's parents described a happy, well-functioning boy, with perhaps a few minor problems in some academic areas. I began to feel that perhaps Miles's teacher had exaggerated his problems. When I finally met Miles, I was more than surprised to find that although he could read adequately, he could not spell even the words required of a second grader, his writing was almost illegible, and he could hardly complete the simplest addition or subtraction problems.

From the moment Miles entered my office, it was apparent that he would rather be anywhere else than with me. He was sullen and unhappy. When I asked him why he had come to see me (often a revealing question to ask an older student), he replied that he had no idea. I believed him, although I have met some youngsters who do know why they have come but refuse to admit it. Miles did not seem to realize that he had a problem and he certainly was less than enthusiastic about coming for help. He claimed to be satisfied with his work, saying he just wanted to be "left alone." I suggested to Miles that we meet four times; then we'd compare notes, so to speak, telling each other what we thought about Miles's need for help and my ability to help him.

That was four years ago. I still don't think Miles's parents are fully accepting of his difficulties, but they have come a long way in understanding his learning problems. They are now reconciled to the fact that Miles should enroll in a modified or slow math program in junior high school, and they are supportive of his outside tutoring. As they have faced Miles's learning difference, he has accepted the reality of his problems with math and spelling. He knows they may last forever, but he recognizes that with effort he can improve his skills.

Following the initial feelings of guilt and anger, disappointment and anxiety are perhaps the most universal feelings that parents have about their children's learning differences. They may wonder whether an offspring will ever go to college or will even finish high school. This may be a particularly hard moment for an ambitious and successful father of a son. Accepting the fact that Jimmy may not be either "Harvard material" or first string on the football team might be more of a blow to Dad's pride than he realizes. How many thousands of Saturday-afternoon hours fathers spend trying to create young athletic stars from unable and unwilling candidates! Parents have wishes and fantasies about their children; it is hard to reconcile them when youngsters don't live up to those expectations.

Acceptance by the family is hard enough, but the hurt may grow when the neighbors learn not only that Jimmy will not go to Harvard but also that he might even need a special class or school for children with learning problems. The special treatment becomes a stigma among the neighborhood children. Since the passage of federal legislation guaranteeing public education for all handicapped children, the term "learning disability" has almost become synonymous with "handicapped." Youngsters with learning disabilities are included in the federal bill as part of the broader category. The "invisible handicap," as it is sometimes called, thus becomes all too apparent, setting Jimmy apart from the neighborhood gang and creating embarrassment for his family. That his handicap doesn't show makes his difference no less obvious to his peers and neighbors.

We profess to respect individual differences, but we are organized to deal with similarities. We expect our children to conform to community norms and to develop just like everyone else on the block. I've been told that in other countries, unlike in the United States, the extended family and neighbors provide more of a support system for handicapped children. This means that the immediate family does not have to face alone the disappointment, pressures, and rejection of raising a nonconforming child.

For some parents, a child's learning problems do not create the shame and resentment talked about thus far. They can, instead, provide the raison d'être for a mother or father, a focus for their energies. Some parents who perhaps have not found their niche in life make a child's learning difference a full-time career. One such man made his son's problems the focal point of the family. He spent more time lobbying for programs in the school district and fund-raising for the special school Peter attended than he did at the office or at home with his family. Lester's mother, too, not only spoke in public at every invitation and devised daily lessons for her son to do, but eventually became a tutor for other youngsters when Lester no longer needed her services. While constructive for the cause and supportive for the child with the handicap, such endeavors may be out of proportion and detrimental to the rest of the family. In psychological terms, this behavior may become a form of overcompensation.

Sisters and brothers have very real problems when a sibling has difficulty learning. All sorts of thoughts and feelings come into play. They may fear that they will turn out like the child with the problem. Often they hear much arguing at home about their sibling's poor grades at school or unfinished homework. When younger sisters and brothers see how distasteful their older sibling finds reading and schoolwork, they may become frightened in anticipation of school. One kindergartner, brought for an evaluation because of his resistance to going to school, said that he hated school "because of the homework." When questioned, he admitted that he had not had any as yet, but that he expected the boom to fall any day. He lived in fear of those long assignments of which he had heard so much at home.

Occasionally, sisters or brothers may feel guilty that they are succeeding in school. Their achievement can become both a responsibility and a burden. The successful child might well fear the possibility of failure, no matter how remote, and his parents' subsequent disappointment in him. He may sense the extent of his parents' investment in him and feel that their approval depends on the number of As on his report card. He may be almost right. Sometimes parents rely too heavily on their successful children to assuage their feelings of inadequacy and frustration with the son or daughter who cannot learn easily.

On a deeper level, all siblings at times experience hatred

toward a sister or brother. When that child turns out to have a learning disability, the other child may feel an enormous amount of guilt and anxiety, since in his mind his wishes created the fact. A poignant example occurred during the much-publicized blackout of 1965. An eight-year-old who was constantly picking on his "dumb little brother" was in big trouble with his mother. She had insisted that he be home at five o'clock as a form of punishment for his fraternal hostility. As he arrived at his front gate, he angrily kicked the telephone pole. At the same instant, the lights went out all over town. His parents later found out that he felt personally responsible for having caused the darkness that paralyzed the East Coast that night. Young children feel that they will be punished for their "bad" feelings and thoughts and they are unable to distinguish between their fantasies and a logical series of events. Thus, having a sibling who has more than his share of problems can be an extra burden for a child. Parents' awareness of the feelings of the other children in the family can help to defuse some of the conflict.

One fifteen-year-old boy confessed to me that he did not want to grow up. He didn't look forward to birthdays and even forgot how old he was at times, claiming to be a year younger than his actual age. He was particularly worried about graduating from high school and going to work. The prospect of independence and a job terrified him. I understood this unusual reaction more easily when I learned that his older brother had had severe problems in school, had been through the drug scene of the sixties, and was still living at home because he was unable to keep a job. Little wonder my young friend was afraid!

A youngster's learning problems affect other members of a family, too. For grandparents living with or even near the family, the generation gap may seem to be ever-widening. One grandmother told me she felt like a fifth wheel, left out of any family discussions about her grandson's problems in school. She never did understand why no one talked about it when she was there. Her grandson seemed all right to her, if somewhat overindulged by his parents, and she couldn't quite see the cause for all the concern. Her husband, a proud grandfather, had been the fourth generation in his family to go to a fine school out west. He refused to believe that his grandson would in all probability not follow suit. Whenever he began to talk about this favorite subject, the rest of the family cringed, but they were unable (and perhaps unwilling) to apprise him of the truth and help him deal with it.

How does a child with a learning difference feel about his own problems and the response of everyone to him? In a word, different! Unless he's a toddler, he usually knows something is wrong long before anyone discusses it with his parents. At school, he applies the lingo of today's youth to himself and thinks of himself as a "mental case" or a "retard." He can't imagine why some things come easily to him, such as drawing and puzzles, while many academic tasks do not. Following a visit to the school psychologist for an evaluation, one child said, "No one told me why they were giving me all those tests. I was scared she'd find out I was retarded."

Scared or not, a youngster knows when he can't read or spell; therefore, he "knows" he's dumb. Other kids in his class agree, calling him "stupid" or "baby," and he believes them. He feels isolated and alone with his problems. It does little good for his parents or his counselors at school to reassure him that he is smart. He knows all too well how he feels! Occasionally, I have made a friendly wager with a child whom I know will emerge as a good student sometime in the future. I tell him that, impossible as it now seems, his teachers and classmates will soon recognize his ability. I stand to lose a good deal of trust if I'm wrong, but I only bet when I'm sure.

Kevin was a nonreader when he moved from Tennessee in the second grade. He was bright and inquisitive, and he excelled in math. As the year progressed, he became disenchanted with his new school and discouraged about his ability to read. Finally he confessed that he hated school and he *never* wanted to learn to read. I made a bet that someday he would even *like* to read when he didn't have to struggle to do so. He didn't believe me at first, sure his dislike of school was forever. It takes a big man to admit he's wrong, but six months later, Kevin came into my office, saying in his lovely

Tennessee drawl, "Mrs. Osman, would you believe I'm beginnin' to like readin'?" I would indeed!

Incidentally, the more intelligent the child, the more intensely he is likely to feel the frustration of a learning difference. He can't understand why he is unable to perform as he knows he should. At six, Amy couldn't write her name or recall how to draw a triangle, although she could recognize and name both when she saw them. She used to stamp her foot in anger, crying, "I always forget it and I knowed it before." She needed a great deal of help to understand that she had a problem but that she could, with good teaching and a lot of effort on her part, learn how to learn and to master some of the things that seemed impossible to her.

"No one understands me" must be the feeling many children have, particularly when no one tells them just what it is that is wrong. Do we, as parents, ever really understand them? Or do our own feelings get in the way? Youngsters who have difficulty learning probably feel much the same way as travelers in a foreign country. You can't read the street signs, you may find the customs strange, and you can't even find a familiar candy bar in the local store. It is important for adults to put themselves in their children's shoes mentally. Imagine yourself trying to accomplish everyday life tasks without the skills and tools you take for granted.

Openness in dealing with what is a family problem is the key. Many families do not share their feelings or thoughts easily. Each member of the group keeps to himself and exchanges few words with the others in the course of a day. People talk only when things have to be done. "Take care of the baby after school." "Go to bed." "Hurry up, I'm leaving!" These may be the only words spoken. One father professed not to understand his son at all. He was considering a special class placement for him, and when I asked how the boy felt about it, he said, "I don't really know. He keeps to himself and I never know what he's thinking. My wife knows him better than I do. Actually, I don't think I know him at all." This father admitted that he had never really encouraged his son to share his feelings with him, perhaps because of his discomfort with his son's problems and his wish to avoid the issue. For many reasons, the adults in a child's world sometimes fail to teach him that feelings are valid and that words exist to express them.

In other families, few subjects are taboo; practically nothing is off-limits. There is a great deal of talking and discussion. Feelings are expressed, sex information is freely dispensed, and even the subject of death can be discussed. But a child's learning differences frequently remain under wraps, classified information, acknowledged only by parents. Some parents recognize this state of affairs, saying that they don't want to call attention to a youngster's problems because "it will make him feel different." Again, I suspect this is more self-protection for parents than real help for the child. In all probability, he feels different anyway.

I can usually tell quite soon when a child's learning difference is a "secret" in the family. I always extend an open invitation to my young clients to bring a friend to an occasional session. Most children love to bring their buddies and proudly show them around the office, making such comments as "This is the game I told you about, and here is where she keeps the candy." Occasionally, though, a child will recoil at the idea of bringing someone along. He doesn't even want his friends to know where he goes on Wednesday afternoons, and he ducks if an acquaintance passes by my street-level office window. Sometimes children desire secrecy even more than their parents, but in most instances, children's attitudes toward coming for help reflect their parents' feelings about it.

All too often, parents' reactions to a child with a learning problem reflect a house divided. From the start, a mother's and father's roles and participation are different. First, a mother gives birth to the infant and often seem clairvoyant about her child's development. No one else sees what she sees as her child grows. And while she may point with pride to those things Johnny does earlier than his sister, she may not be quite as eager to mention her doubts and fears, so fathers may not encounter the reality of a youngster's difficulties until he is in school.

Then, too, school conferences are usually scheduled during the school day. If a husband's schedule is less flexible than his wife's, the child's mother may have to go alone to those painful meetings at school. She cannot share her concern with her husband at that moment, and suppertime is obviously not the right time either. It is probably late at night before the children are in bed and parents can be alone. By then, both are tired and in no mood to discuss problems. Besides, the husband might say he's had enough at the office. His response to his wife's report of the conference may be an unsympathetic reminder that he must have been like his son when he was a boy. He was slow in reading and recalls having been "bored to death" in school. Now he's doing well enough. Billy will too; just give him time. A few minutes later, his wife may be the only one still awake in the house, alone with her feelings and her fears about Billy.

One father I knew had unrealistic expectations for his son, refusing to believe that he couldn't achieve like everyone else. "He could do it if he tried." He had convinced himself that Roger would catch up in high school. He had little patience with his wife's more realistic appraisal of Roger and with her efforts to help him. In fact, he rather resented the time she spent with Roger's homework and even suspected that she might have created Roger's disability by spoiling him. His resentment put an additional strain on his relationship with his wife and drove him further away from his son. Perhaps, too, Roger's experiences reminded him of his own painful school years, and it was hard to think of them again.

Fathers often exclude themselves from a child's life at school, particularly when there is a problem. Many families still maintain the attitude that "Mother is in charge of school matters." Mother may have no choice but to assume the responsibility for the child's difficulties, even to the point of making all decisions that come up—whether he should be evaluated, tutored, or sent to a special school or camp. Mother helps him with homework and soon becomes his advocate and chief supporter. Mother and child become more of a team than ever before, and the father is in the outfield.

This doesn't have to happen. It may take longer for a father to understand and accept a child's learning difficulties if he is not part of the initial meetings, but with help and his wife's wish to include him, it can be done. I have found that when a mother and the professionals involved take the time to include the father in the planning and carrying out of programs, he can be a most effective member of the team. Since many school systems tend to be old-fashioned, fathers' interventions often carry more weight. In fact, when it comes to the legal aspects of procuring special services and programs, many fathers have had to become instant lawyers for their children.

Even with their later or lesser participation, fathers do have a special role for their children with learning differences. First, they are important models, particularly for their sons. A boy admires his father, whether or not his father is a good athlete and/or a success in the adult world. A role model is crucial for a growing child with learning problems. A boy needs to know he will grow up to be a whole man, despite his learning differences or other problems. A father's tacit acceptance makes this process easier and more comfortable. Conversely, fathers can all too easily make healthy growth impossible if they think of their children as incompetent and unable to measure up to their expectations.

Fathers can also be involved directly with their children's education. Many fathers may have a welcome talent for helping a child with homework. Frequently, mothers are too tired and harassed by homework time. They have been doing things with and for their children all day long, and their patience is wearing thin. If Father can take a fresh look at Jimmy and be objective and helpful in his approach, there is much to be gained for both father and son. Above all, a husband's support and willingness to share the responsibility with his wife bring a family closer together. Parents ought to look at who does what best and divide the educational chores accordingly.

Recently, I invited some dyslexic high school students to speak to a class of graduate students in special education. The teenage panelists were asked how they felt about their learning differences and what had been most helpful to them during their difficult years. One boy told the group how supportive his father had been while he struggled through school. He said he couldn't have made it without his father's understanding. A colleague who was present recalled how far this father had come in coping with his son's learning problems. When first told of the difficulty his son was having, way back when the child was in in second grade, the father responded with violent anger and denial. Through the years, the child's educational therapist had helped him see how effective he could be in helping his son. He became an ardent supporter of the rights and programs for the learning-disabled children in his community and deeply involved with his own son. Their relationship went far beyond the school situation and became mutually rewarding.

Once parents understand what is wrong with their child and can acknowledge how they feel about his problems, they can alleviate a significant amount of the child's anxiety by explaining the problem to him as honestly as possible. Children need to know the truth in language they can understand. Parents should relieve youngsters of the guilt that arises from not feeling smart—or not being the kind of people others would want them to be. With acceptance and support at home, they can better face what may often appear to be a teasing or hostile world. They'll be reassured that their troubles can't be so terrible if these troubles can be discussed, and they'll be less likely to imagine frightening reasons for their differences. A child may find unexpected allies in his brothers and sisters if they are in the know and understand what really is wrong. The whole family will benefit from talking about this formerly taboo subject.

Parents must also tell a child what is *right* with him. There is always something to praise. One part of a child's life—as student, athlete, or artist—should not become all-important to anyone. After all, he is a child and a person too. A child must know that somebody cares about *all* of him, not just his learning skills, in order for him to develop trust in others and faith in himself.

Chapter 3

Life
at Home

"Jimmy, what *is* taking you so long? You're going to be late for school again. I give up! Why can't you ever be on time?"

The time is eight-thirty on a Tuesday morning, and everyone at the Merlins' is angry at Jimmy. Mother was supposed to leave for work ten minutes ago, but she has to wait to take Jimmy and his older sister, Susan, to school on her way to work. Jennie, who is a preschooler, will go to the day-care center. Susan is also angry with Jimmy. It's not her turn to walk the dog. Mrs. Merlin has been through this unpleasant scene every weekday morning since school began in September, and nothing seems to change. Why is Jimmy always so poky? Her irritation with him rises when she remembers that she didn't sleep well last night because of him. Jimmy had come into his parents' room in the middle of the night, complaining that he was scared. "At nine, he's too old for that," his father said. "Why does he demand so much time and attention—so much more than either of the other two children?"

Upstairs, Jimmy is oblivious to the tension he's created below. He's still in his pajamas, but he did get out of bed. He's watching his goldfish chase each other in the bowl. He comes to with a start when he hears the urgency in his mother's voice, and he remembers unhappily that this is another school day. Where did his shoes go? They were here last night. And one leg of his pants is turned inside out, and he can't seem to straighten it out. Now Mother is angry again. Why does this always happen to him? It's so hard getting started each day! Later that afternoon, Mrs. Merlin is fixing dinner in the kitchen and Susan is trying to talk to a friend on the telephone. It's not easy with Jimmy screaming at his little sister for dropping her magnet in his fishbowl. Mother has a tense, grim expression on her face. She has had a hard day and Jimmy hasn't made it any easier. He raided the refrigerator before she came home from work, spilling the orange juice, and then he left the refrigerator door open. A little while later, Mrs. Merlin had to rescue the puppy from his tight clutches. She had known from the moment Jimmy woke up that this was going to be another of his "bad days." Why do his difficult times seem to affect the mood of the entire household? Susan put the whole situation in perspective when she said, "It sure is different around here when that brat is out of the house!"

Why is it that in so many homes children with learning differences seem to be the catalysts for tension and chaos? Some of the reasons undoubtedly lie within the children themselves. Their anxieties and unpredictable outbursts seem impossible to control. They tend to dawdle, to be disorganized, and to be unaware of the consequence of their actions. They don't mean to squeeze the puppy too tightly or to push the glass pane out of the door. But these are all behaviors associated with their learning differences. There's a small children's book entitled *One Day Everything Went Wrong*, [1] and all too often this seems to be the story of these youngsters' lives.

Specialists have argued, and some research has shown, that the families of learning-disabled children tend to be more chaotic and disorganized than other families—perhaps even before the child with the problem arrived on the scene. Some have said that the child with problems only adds to family patterns already in existence. Which comes first is a moot point. In any case, the problems create a vicious cycle with the youngster contributing to the tension and frustration in the family, and the atmosphere at home augmenting the confusion and ultimate rejection of the child. He may in fact be held responsible for more chaos than even he could create.

The day at the Merlins I have just described will seem all too familiar to many readers. But is it really necessary? Can nothing be done to alleviate the tension and aggravation that exist? Though it is difficult for families to change their patterns of living, no one in a family may really have tried to make things different. Perhaps a child's dawdling and his annoying habits are taken for granted, or maybe it just seems easier to live with the status quo than to recognize the possibilities for improvement and change.

It is always hard to change habits; today, with two working parents in many families, it becomes harder for parents to plan together. Too often, family members pass one another in the kitchen on the way to and from work or school. And except for psychological counseling, which is inaccessible to many because of the expense, parents receive little guidance and training in parenting difficult children. Parents are expected to do what comes naturally, but at best this isn't easy. It's even harder when youngsters have problems.

Families develop different ways of living with children whose learning problems affect their behavior. Chaos and turmoil comprise only one of the life styles. In Jimmy's family, his presence seemed to charge the atmosphere. Much of the tension, arguing, and excitement revolved around him. Since his sisters had not been told enough about his problems, they thought he misbehaved deliberately, and they resented him. Jimmy felt their resentment and in turn became so accustomed to his role that he, too, accepted it as a natural part of life. He saw himself as the family troublemaker and never expected anything to change.

A key word for a family in this situation might be *organization*. First, Jimmy might have to get up fifteen minutes or so earlier in the morning, when his mother or father could be on hand to keep him moving. To help him dress, his mother or father could lay the clothing of his choice out for him the night before, and breakfast could be toast and cheese or some other finger food to eat on the way to school. Then there might be a storage box or shelf near the front door for boots and schoolbooks, for easier grabbing on the way out. In other words, if we know that Jimmy has a hard time organizing his belongings and his time, we should realize that structure must come from the outside. Realistically, Jimmy's parents could not depend on Jimmy to dress himself, feed his goldfish, make his bed, eat breakfast, and gather his schoolbooks in time to leave for school with his mother and sister.

His parents must therefore provide the support and order in his world until such time as he can manage it himself.

Parents sometimes refuse to help their children with such routine tasks as dressing on the basis that they must learn to be independent, to function on their own. "We mustn't baby him," or "He can do it if he tries," they will say. However, youngsters with learning differences and/or behavioral problems can learn more efficiently from a good example than from criticism and punishment for what they did wrong. Most of us do. Psychologists of the behaviorist school claim that punishment can actually serve to reinforce undesirable behavior. Establishing the habit of good organization by example will teach a child more than a string of verbal directives.

The scientific axiom "For every action there is a reaction" applies to human beings as well as to physics. I am reminded of Henry, who at the age of ten got attention at home and at school by being irritating and annoying. He interrupted every conversation, made peculiar noises when people were trying to read, and was a "hands-on" child, always touching and annoying other children. No one took any notice of him when he was good—at least that's the way it looked to him—so he made sure he was noticed. His need for recognition and attention seemed insatiable. His mother in turn became angry, then guilty because of her hostile feelings toward him, and the vicious cycle went on and on. Henry knew when his mother was upset with him, although he denied that it affected him. "It doesn't bother me when my mother cries," he said. "It just makes me cry too."

Finally I helped Henry's mother to see that she need not feel guilty; her anger was a natural reaction to an irritating situation. But it was time to help Henry reconstruct his role in the family. He had to learn that negative behavior would no longer pay off with Mother's attention, and that acceptable behavior could be more richly rewarded.

Henry happened to be the only child in his family with a learning disability, but when more than one child has one—and this is so often the case—the family problems are different. On the one hand, misery loves company, and mutual understanding and bonds may develop between the affected children. No child stands out in the family as being different, and parents may be able to enforce a more uniform standard of behavior. Parents in one family with five learning-disabled children geared the pace and activities of family life to the capabilities of their youngsters, so no one felt out of step. The children might have missed the excitement of an occasional parade or community picnic, but they were calmer and happier at home.

I have no doubt that it requires a great deal of stamina and patience for parents to provide the support and guidance for one, let alone many, special children. Parents can run out of steam and grow more impatient as more children show signs of having problems. As one father groaned when his third child was diagnosed as learning-disabled in kindergarten, "I'm too old to go through this again." He managed, though, and that daughter is now a teacher.

But we all have to remember that children's roles vary significantly. In some families, the child with the problems unwittingly becomes the scapegoat, the butt of everyone's anger and hostility. One mother told me, "The other children in the family pick on Russell, but there doesn't seem to be much we can do about it. We try to tell them to stop, but nothing seems to work."

Russell was almost eleven, the middle child in his family and the only boy. His older sister admitted that she thought he was stupid, and she told him so at every opportunity. Her parents agreed that she was very hard on Russell, but they didn't know how to help. Russell's younger sister, who was only six, was a tease. She took his precious possessions and wouldn't give them back when he asked. Then after Russell hit her, she'd yell and run to tell their mother. She knew what would happen. "He should know better," his parents would say as they meted out the punishment. "She's just a baby."

Russell thought he was picked on more than his sisters, but he said it was because he always did "bad things." He had begun to accept the fact that he couldn't do anything right and that when his big sister called him a "retard," she wasn't far wrong. He used to deprecate himself, as if to beat her to the punch, saying "I'm dumb" or "I rot," which upset his family even more. Wistfully Russell recalled as the best thing that ever happened to him the time his father woke him up late at night to praise him for having been so good that day.

Dinnertime was usually not fun for Russell either. He never seemed to know what anyone was talking about, and when he asked a question, the family either ignored him or responded with anger. Russell's dad confessed that his son annoyed him at the table because his remarks were "usually irrelevant or two subjects behind." During one meal, his older sister complained about the way he was eating and the fact that he had made her late for school again. Then his mother told Russell his room was such a mess she couldn't get in to clean it. He finally left the table, too upset to eat.

In discussing Russell's role in the family, his parents seemed surprised to hear me say that he had become a full-fledged scapegoat, a foil for everyone's frustrations. Only Russell's father seemed slightly aware that Russell was having a difficult time at home. Perhaps unconsciously, everyone in the family had chosen the weakest link in the chain—namely Russell—to bear the brunt of their angry feelings. Russell's parents began to see the anger and frustration that had been directed at Russell and realized what these attitudes were doing to all of them. It is a well-known tenet in family therapy that the identified patient may not be at the root of the problem at all, but may merely be the most convenient target. Persons with learning differences often seem particularly vulnerable to scapegoating as a consequence of their deficient coping abilities and their weak self-image.

I tried to help Russell's mother see that when she expected him to act his age in the face of his sister's teasing, she was demanding more maturity of him than he had. She was critical of him for getting down to his sister's level, but maybe that is really where he was. A child's learning difference frequently reflects a maturational lag in behavior as well as in learning, and Russell was probably at the same stage of maturity educationally and behaviorally as his six-year-old sister, despite his larger shoe size and his higher grade in school. (Actually, she had already surpassed him in reading skills.)

When a youngster is the scapegoat in a family, it is often with the unconscious consent of all the family, even those who profess to be supportive. Russell's parents began to gain a better understanding of the family dynamics, but it became apparent that Russell required more than just understanding and passive acceptance from his family. He needed his parents' active support. I suggested that Russell's mother try to come to Russell's defense in some of his many battles with his sisters, if there was even the slightest reason for doing so, in hopes of changing the longstanding pattern of their attacks.

It worked. When Russell's mother scolded his younger sister for using his record player without his permission, everyone was shocked. Russell told me he couldn't believe his ears. But even that wasn't enough. Part of the change had to come from Russell. He needed help in learning to assert himself in a positive way rather than provoking his sisters needlessly. This is usually the more difficult aspect to change. As I pointed out, a child's destructive patterns can become his way of gaining recognition and attention, even if it is the wrong kind. "It's better to be picked on than never to be noticed at all" seems to be the philosophy of many children.

Actions speak louder than words. Merely explaining to children that they are provoking and stirring things up unnecessarily at home probably won't convince them. Chances are they won't even know what their parents are talking about. On the other hand, rewarding any honest effort with recognition and praise is a far better way to effect a change. Occasionally, when this technique is suggested, a parent will say, "I tried that once, but it didn't work." Granted, it will take more than once for a child to unlearn inappropriate behavior. It took him a lifetime to learn it, and there's no shortcut to changing his ways. We can't expect magic, but if we begin with one small change in behavior and gradually increase our expectations, the child will see that success is attainable. For example, if he is on time for dinner four out of five nights, you might have some small reward waiting for him at the end of the week.

Sometimes role-playing between parent and child or professional and child is one way for a youngster to understand concretely what he is doing that is unacceptable to others. Dr. Richard Gardner, a proponent of this technique, describes the process in his book *Psychotherapeutic Approaches to the Resistant Child*.[2] In essence, he and the child create a story or play script to illustrate the undesirable behavior as well as the hoped-for transformation. If your child has difficulty thinking conceptually, such a concrete, graphic illustration may help him change even the most firmly entrenched of inappropriate habits.

Timing is important. You can't teach a child alternate ways of acting at the height of a dispute or conflict. Once the tension is over and the air is cleared, though, it may be possible to help a child understand what provoked the argument in the first place. As parents, we sometimes blame a youngster for an argument or angry scene when our own mood or frustration may have caused the conflict. The way we respond to our children at any given time is directly related to the way we feel about ourselves. If we are in a time of emotional stress, it may well be that we have to step back to see more objectively what it is that caused us to be vulnerable to a child's onslaught or more susceptible than usual to a quarrel.

If we were responsible, a little honest confession might be called for. Assuming at least partial responsibility alleviates some of the child's inevitable guilt and helps him see that his parents are human too. It is also a fact that children are not as fragile as they look. Parents can make many mistakes and say some regrettable things that youngsters will tolerate well, so long as there is honesty between them.

I'm reminded of the time a mother lost her temper at the end of a long day and slapped a child in the face for a minor infraction. She felt great remorse and guilt, so she hugged her little boy and tearfully apologized. He began to jump up and down on the bed, shouting gleefully, "You're sorry, I'm sorry, we're both sorry!" In other words, honest expression of feeling can clear the air faster than any long-winded discussion.

Another and perhaps more important way to stop scapegoating is to help the victim see his role in the family relationships. There cannot be a victim without his acquiescence and consent. Why does a child accept this role in the first place? How does he feel about himself that he allows himself to bear the brunt of others' hostility and teasing? We can't know precisely how children feel, but it must be hard to have healthy self-esteem when they are exposed to failure and frustration in school and disappointment and deprecation at home. Too frequently they feel they get what they deserve when they are scapegoated. Parents may have to take a good long look at their relationship with a child to help the child see his role in his family's treatment of him.

The flip side of being scapegoated is to be overly indulged. In some families, everyone seems to try to compensate the child for his impairment by overindulging and overprotecting him. The child with the problem becomes the focus of everyone's attention and energy. To an observer, he would appear to be the favorite child. While his siblings grow up with little coddling, he is catered to and little or nothing is asked of him.

One mother seemed to spend every waking moment doing things for her son, chauffeuring him to swimming lessons, tutors, and to the neighborhood toy store for presents. The rest of the family was lucky if they saw her over a pot-luck supper. Tom's father tried to put things into perspective, accusing his wife of spoiling Tom and admitting that he resented all the time and attention given to the child. Mother and son had in effect become a twosome, and he felt excluded. His wife was annoyed, claiming that he was unsympathetic to his son's difficulties. The other children in the family also felt that Tom was spoiled. They resented the privileges and special attention to which only Tom seemed entitled, and they couldn't understand the reasons for their mother's indulgence.

The family finally sought professional help to try to reassess the priorities in the family. How much energy did Tom's mother really have to expend, and how much of her busywork was necessary for Tom's development and well-being? Parents who overprotect their children are not a homogeneous group, but they do have one thing in common—namely, that they do more for their children than the reality of the situation requires.

Some parents overprotect children because of their own insecurity or sense of inadequacy. By carefully paving the way for a youngster, parents feel they will spare him some of the discomfort and anxiety to which they themselves are vulnerable. It is also true that parents' anger or disappointment with a child may be more easily disguised when they are doing special favors for him. The attention and gifts become tangible evidence of their devotion and love. Many parents who feel blame for their children's disorders assume more than their share of the responsibility for their children's actions. Related to this, too, may be a parent's guilt for having produced a youngster with real or imagined damage. Through selflessness and protection of the child above and beyond the call of duty, they attempt to assuage some of the guilt.

Parental overprotection has two aspects. One is the need to dominate and control the child; the other is excessive permissiveness and indulgence. A parent may dominate and overindulge a youngster at the same time, though one behavior does not necessarily accompany the other. Barbara was a pretty and compliant twelve-year-old whose mother continued to assume most of the responsibility for her daughter's daily life. Having seen how ineptly Barbara planned her time, even for such simple tasks as bathing and dressing, her mother thought she was doing Barbara a favor when she planned even those activities for her. Moreover, since she filled Barbara's days with lessons and appointments, she ensured that Barbara had little time in which to have to handle the real world of childhood. She kept Barbara out of situations in which she might have difficulty, thus making Barbara's disabilities appear less significant, hardly even noticeable.

With all this supervision, Barbara was not able to develop her capabilities, even in those areas where she might have achieved. She passively accepted the identity her mother had created for her, becoming increasingly dependent on her parents. As time went on, she couldn't or wouldn't move without their guidance. Eventually, Barbara's parents began to worry about her future life without them. How could she possibly manage? She relied on them for everything. In effect, all three had become enslaved by the dependency they had helped to create.

Though it is important for parents to give support when it is needed, it is equally important to encourage a child to try his wings. Youngsters with learning differences *do* tend to be dependent in some areas longer than their siblings. But their parents need to be especially patient while the children try, fail, and try again. Youngsters can only become independent, self-reliant, and well-functioning adults if they are encouraged and supported in their efforts to grow. Every parent knows it is easier and more efficient to assume the responsibility for many of the tasks of childhood, but it is a disservice to the youngsters who need to become autonomous.

This advice is often more easily given than followed. Fostering independence in a child for whom learning does not come easily would tax the patience of Job. It is twice as hard to teach a child with poor coordination to ride a two-wheeler, and teaching an impulsive youngster to cross a busy thoroughfare only on the green light is undeniably frustrating. And even when they have taught their children all they can, parents may be nervous about giving a child freedom to move into a potentially dangerous situation. He may be easily distracted and forget to look where he is going—just once. There is a fine line between protecting a child from a situation he is not ready to handle and overprotecting him. Parents need insight, courage, a sense of humor, and a great deal of patience to cope with their children's trials and errors in the process of learning and living.

The other characteristic of overprotection—excessive indulgence and permissiveness—usually occurs with parents who are either submissive themselves or guilty about their children's problems. Mike was nine, and although he couldn't read or ride a bicycle yet, he surely had his parents under his thumb. Because of their concern and sympathy for Mike, his parents couldn't do enough for him. His every wish was their command; rules of the house did not apply to him. He could watch TV while his brother could not, and he alone ignored the established bedtime, going to bed whenever he wished. He had no assigned chores either. He complained so about responsibility that it was easier for his parents to do his jobs or to assign them to the other children. Mike became more demanding as he grew older, and his parents adopted an attitude of peace at any price. It was simpler to appease him than to deal with his explosions and bad moods. Mike was a masterful manipulator at home, but he became unduly upset when confronted with the demands of the world outside. He could not tolerate any denial of his wants and gradually withdrew from any contacts that would frustrate him. To function adequately in an adult world, Mike—like all youngsters—needed to develop a feeling of competence. When children are given everything they want, they are robbed of this opportunity.

By the time a child reaches adolescence, new and special problems arise, though many of the earlier symptoms of the child's learning difference might have disappeared. In all probability, he is no longer as obviously hyperactive as he once was; he may even be able to read the newspaper. But the discrepancy between his behavior and the expectations for someone of his age may appear wider than ever to those who know him well.

Among the most conspicuous attributes of adolescents with learning differences are their impulsivity and a need for immediate gratification, which inhibit good judgment; their shortsightedness, which limits their goals and plans for the future, and their suggestibility, which makes them prey to misguided leadership. These budding adults tend to remain egocentric, concerned only with themselves and their problems, and their conversation may be repetitive and dull. They make little constructive use of their spare time and seem to lack the resources to amuse themselves. As a result, they tend to rely on their parents for companionship. One eighteen-year-old's favorite activity was to putter in the kitchen with her mother. Her mother, recognizing Liz's need to fill empty hours, obliged as often as she could, but she had a full-time job and felt burdened by the extra time spent among the pots and pans.

The adolescent period can be particularly difficult for a child who has been overprotected in his youth. He will often lack the skills essential for independence. His six-foot frame may hide the little boy who shuns responsibility inside. He still needs to be told what to do. However, like most adolescents, he probably resents the assistance and is in more of a bind than most of his peers, since his needs are in conflict with his aspirations. He may also be confused by the mixed messages he is receiving from his parents. He is regarded as a child in need of supervision, but is expected to be an adult. Many parents are afraid of their teenagers learning to drive, yet they want them to get part-time jobs to foster independence. Their ambivalence only increases the stress for the youngster.

To some degree, all adolescents are caught between the lures of adulthood and the comforts of childhood. But adolescence presents special problems for parents too. While it is true that adolescents with learning differences need independence, as do all teenagers, they also require more support and guidance than their peers. Their social and sexual relationships may also be immature. Some may be afraid to indulge in heterosexual relationships, while others may indulge too freely because of their desire for acceptance. They may need help in handling dates and telephone conversations appropriately, and even in knowing how to travel alone. Assistance may also be required in filling out job applications. All this takes time and patience.

Many parents become weary of teenage problems and discouraged about the results of their teaching. While a child is young, his parents feel there is time to remediate his disability and help him outgrow his differences. But by the teen years time is running out. Suddenly he's a young adult—and he *still* has problems. But at this stage it is more important than ever that parents not allow their own anxieties to interfere with their teenagers' acquisition of skills necessary to succeed in their world. Parents need the courage to demand responsibility of their young adults and to say no when it is indicated. This may well be their last chance to provide their offspring with the tools they need for independence. On the other hand, the adolescent spends less time at home and more time with his peers. As a result, he is less available for parental guidance.

I don't want to overstress the negatives and the difficulties that young children with learning differences present to their families. Moreover, I do not intend to convey the impression that a youngster with a learning problem necessarily assumes a destructive or neurotic role in his family. In many homes, he is an integral, contributing member of the family, loved and respected by all. Indeed, he has much to teach others about the traits of perseverence, patience, and determination to succeed.

Many of the negative feelings discussed in this section— sibling rivalry, the denial of problems, and the frustration inherent in raising a family—occur in *all* families. All part of the growing process and living together under one roof, these perfectly natural feelings are handled with equanimity and understanding in some families. Though I have observed many such families with interest and admiration, trying to understand just what it is they do that works so well, I've found no standard formula or life style. Some of the families live on farms, others in large cities or in the suburbs. They can be one-parent families or foster homes. Undoubtedly there is an element of luck, but some parents seem particularly sensitive and tuned in to the needs of their children. Whether or not their children have problems, these parents are able to provide an environment that is comfortable, accepting, and nurturing for all the family.

One such family, the Langs, seemed to pay little attention to their daughter's learning difference. They provided tutoring for Susie after school, but they did not seem overly concerned about her academic progress, nor did they ever ask what occurred during her lessons. In contrast with many parents of youngsters who come for help, I had little or no contact with the Langs. They rarely phoned and almost never canceled appointments; they allowed Susie to walk to my office alone, even in the rain. Usually I would take this behavior as indicative of parental uninterest or lack of involvement. But it became obvious that Susie had their love and respect, and she seemed to know just what she could expect from her family. She relied on them for help when she felt it was needed, but she was encouraged to be independent and to do for herself whenever possible. She was treated as a normal youngster with recognizable learning problems that could be tolerated and coped with at home. Above all, her parents did not seem to need Susie's successes for their own gratification or feeling of accomplishment.

The Langs understood that all children need standards and expectations. Their child with a learning problem was no different. We do a child no favor when we take pity on him because of his problems and make no demands on him. He needs to know that his parents and teachers expect as much of him as he is capable of handling. We may, for example, not be able to insist on a neat, tidy room if disorganization is one of his problems, but we can try to maintain the standard by *helping* him achieve it. Help a child help himself and he'll become his own master.

Many parents have learned through experience how to deal beautifully with their learning-disabled children. Routines, demands of time, reward and punishment, and TV scheduling are a few of the problem areas with which they have learned to cope. A few suggestions culled from parents' experiences are offered here, in the hopes of making daily living somewhat easier.

Time and attention are commodities very much needed by youngsters with learning differences, but often in busy families there's not enough to go around. Children with learning problems need more parental time than their sisters and brothers do, though, because the basic rules of living may not come easily. Then, too, there may be more problems and unhappy times to discuss. A special time might be set aside for the much-needed reading help and for a sharing of the day's happenings. One boy counted on ten minutes with his father before bedtime to talk about "life and stuff." This became known as their "life and stuff" time together. Of course, Mother could take over occasionally when Father wasn't available or in the mood. But someone who cared had to be there for him. And it ensured his parents a better night's sleep and a more contented child. It was worth it!

Instructions and directives are often misunderstood or not heard at all. We can't assume that a child will know and understand directions after he's been told once, particularly if one eye is on the TV or if he is halfway out the door. Some youngsters with learning differences understand and process information rather slowly, and instructions said quickly get lost en route. Parents must take their children's less efficient listening into account and be particularly precise and clear in their explanations.

Raymond had been told to meet his mother at the store to select a new bicycle for his thirteenth birthday. He remembered his birthday and the bicycle, but he forgot where his mother said to meet him and when. He was devastated when he missed the chance to choose his own present. To avoid this scene, his mother might have written the instructions and clipped them to his notebook or tucked them inside his pocket. Even if Raymond had been younger and couldn't read the words, the paper alone might have provided the needed reminder. Eventually Raymond learned to walk around with a pocketful of directives and no longer missed the important events in his life.

Routines are crucial for children with learning differences. They provide the stability and needed structure for youngsters who otherwise may seem lost in time and space. A special time for homework, TV, and dinner will take the guesswork out of living. While regularity may seem monotonous to many of us, it is reassuring for children who cannot handle change and uncertainty well.

Merely telling a child to come home at six for dinner may not necessarily bring him back on time if he tends to be unconscious of the clock, but providing him with a watch with an alarm might work. Or, a phone call to the neighbors, if that is where he is, could serve as a reminder that it is almost dinner time and he'd better start for home. Family life will be calmer and less fraught with tension if you can avoid a last-minute search for an absent-minded child.

Consistency in handling is very desirable, but rarely possible, as most parents know. The level of strictness or permissiveness at home will vary from family to family, but as long as a child knows the basic rules and what he can rely on, he should have fewer tantrums. You might even enumerate the few strict rules that cannot be broken at home by drawings or writing, in anticipation of their being "forgotten." Parents frequently feel unsure of their stand on an issue, but it will give a child a sense of security when he knows that his parents are the authority figures. Children think they want power, but it scares them when they become omnipotent.

Discipline isn't easy. "Nothing works. We can't get through to him" is a comment frequently heard. A child with learning problems is often hard to teach; no punishment seems to make an impression. Generally, a technique of anticipation and prevention is more effective than criticism or punishment after the fact. But parents can't always prevent the crime. A timeout or cooling-off period in a child's room might not teach him the desired behavior, but it will give his parents and family some temporary relief. Granted that even an occasional spanking won't be the end of the world, as a form of punishment it doesn't accomplish much. It is just another negative reinforcer, possibly even encouraging the undesirable behavior. As mentioned before, negative attention seems more attractive to many children than none at all.

Teasing or threats, though, are not just ineffectual; they are highly destructive. Teasing is really an expression of anger said with a smile, and most children quickly become aware of the underlying feelings. One father thought his son was a poor sport when he couldn't take the barbs thrown jokingly across the dinner table. He had not realized how much hostility tipped each arrow until we discussed it.

When serious disciplinary action is required for a basic infraction of a rule, parents need to think long and hard to make the punishment fit the crime. A punishment of long duration, such as no television for a month, will quickly lose its effect. By the middle of that period, the child will remember the punishment but not what it was for. Knowing your child and what pleasures he looks forward to most gives you some leverage. A warning that a trip to the circus can easily be canceled if unacceptable behavior continues is usually sufficient—if the child knows his parents mean what they say. Of course we must assume that the child is able to control the behavior in question.

Special privileges are not always earned. "Why can Jimmy watch TV and I can't?" "How come Tommy doesn't have to stay at the table and I do? It's not fair." Such comments are heard in every house, but become more poignant in families where one child has problems. Equal treatment is not necessarily fair. "To each according to his need" might be a more appropriate slogan.

When siblings ask why their sister or brother gets special treatment, an honest explanation is called for. Siblings should recognize that there are some things Jimmy and Susie require and some things they cannot do, but Jimmy and Susie will be called upon to do what they can. If parents can learn to live with the concept that equality isn't necessarily fair and that meeting individual needs is, so will other members of the family.

TV scheduling becomes a problem in many homes, and parents of children with reading problems often take a somewhat moralistic view of television: "Turn off the boob tube and pick up a book!" However, if Johnny has had a stressful day and reading is a chore, perhaps he needs to relax before going to bed. TV at the end of the day (or right before dinner) can afford a respite from the pressures he has been under. If it doesn't interfere with the family's schedule, perhaps he should be allowed some viewing time, even if it's not educational. This doesn't mean that his brother, an A student who needs prodding to finish his homework, should be permitted the same privilege. Tough on parents? You bet!

Organizing and scheduling are often hard for adolescents in any family. Many seem to think they can accomplish more in ten minutes—after those long phone calls and their favorite TV show —than any human being can do in an hour. They somehow never get to that dreaded homework until amost midnight, and then Mom and Dad are too tired to be sympathetic. One fifteen-year-old girl came up with her own solution one day. She listed all the things she had to do after school—"bathe, write a composition, brush the dog, call Grandmother and two friends, and finish my math." Then she listed them in the order in which she planned to do them and tried to estimate the time allotted for each. She interspersed the phone calls among the chores, and her scheduling worked fairly well. The dog didn't get brushed and the bath had to be hurried, but she was proud of her system and she had become the master of her own time.

A few simple possessions can help with this organization. Most can be made easily at home and should make life easier for a lot of families.

1. *His own bulletin board* or funny signs to remind a youngster of schedules or special appointments. These can be used to reinforce established routines. A section devoted to emergency numbers, thoughts for the day, and household assignments might be useful. One family even had a sign-out sheet for parents and children posted in the kitchen, with the message "I am at _____Will be back at _____."

2. *Magnets* for notes on the refrigerator door or his bathroom mirror. These hold brief messages and reminders of times and dates of activities. One family left all telephone messages on the refrigerator door. It became the central clearinghouse where everyone looked when returning home. That way no one forgot to tell Mother or Father who called.

3. *His own key* on a string, and a special hook in his room on which to hang it. It won't get lost so quickly, and he'll be able to get into the house after school—if he remembers to take it!

4. *Name tapes* aren't babyish, even for adolescents, if they can prevent a trip to the lost-and-found for the jacket and sweater left at school. They will help him stay organized, and will prevent innumerable scoldings.

5. *Eyeglass cases and notebooks* that are well marked with the child's name and address will accomplish the same as name tapes.

6. *Open shelves* in his room to keep possessions off the floor. It's hard for some youngsters to put things away, but open shelves might present a reasonable alternative for under the bed. *Freaky Friday*[3] by Mary Rodgers, a novel that presents a weird twist on parent-child relationships, might give you an interesting perspective on how your teenager sees your comments about his room.

7. *Compartmentalized or divided drawers* are good for faster retrieving of articles needed for school in the morning.

There must be hundreds of other suggestions for more peaceful living with children. You can add to the list those items and ideas that will make life easier for your family. It only takes a little thought. Now, what about you, the children's parents?

Care and treatment of parents is perhaps most important of all. You need relief too. It is not easy to be with people no higher than your waist all day, every day, and a youngster with problems may be much more active and more difficult. You cannot possibly be available to him at all times; it's not even good for him. He won't learn to relate to other adults if you are the only ones he knows. Find a willing grandmother, an aunt, or a local baby sitter to relieve you at regular intervals. You'll come home refreshed and better able to care for your child. Parents of children with learning problems often feel guilty about leaving their child with others. True, he may be hard to handle, but there must be someone who can cope with him.

To sum up, youngsters with learning differences require what all children need, although perhaps more of it. They need to feel loved and accepted. However, it may not be as easy to have kindly feelings toward a child whose moods, judgment, and sense of timing may be off-kilter so much of the time. At times parents understandably feel anger, anxiety, frustration, and fatigue. At such moments, it is hard to be patient. Children with learning differences often seem the most unlovable when they need to be loved the most. Therein lies the challenge for parents, brothers, and sisters! At the same time, parents should not be made to feel guilty or responsible for their children's problems. They, too, need understanding and help. Too often their plight evokes more criticism than compassion from professionals, relatives, and friends who blame them for their children's aberrant behavior. This criticism is unwarranted.

Most parents do the very best they can for their youngsters, and they are deserving of support and help from others. It is not easy to be the parent of a child with a learning difference. Parents should treat themselves to some of the love and understanding they work so hard to provide for their children. The kids will benefit too.

Chapter 4

The Social Connection

People usually think of a learning difference as just that—a problem with learning. But learning encompasses much more than the three Rs. From infancy on, most children begin to learn the important skill of living with others—that is, social perception and interpersonal behavior. A baby soon learns the sound of his mother's voice and "reads" her facial expression as well as her touch. He senses when she is loving and when she feels angry or impatient. This awareness and his recognition of himself as a being distinct from those around him gradually enable him to become his own person. Only then can he interact with others. This is a crucial part of his learning, influencing his behavior all his life. Too often for a child with learning problems, the social aspect of his life represents a much more devastating and prolonged failure than his poor grade in reading.

We know from the study of child development that children move from an egocentric existence toward socialization and companionship with others within the first three years of life, well before they enter school. Newborn infants have a selfish and narcissistic outlook on the world: other people matter only in relation to themselves. If babies' thoughts were expressed in language, those words might be "What can you do for me *now?*" Later toddlers perceive others as things or objects, to be used and pushed around at will. Then, as preschoolers, most tots begin to find that it pays to relate to other children. They gain a helper in building block towers or even in performing some mischief. The partnership is secondary to the activity and lasts only as long as it takes to complete the task. Finally, by the time they enter elementary school, most children have learned to view their peers as individuals with whom they can compete and share possessions, and to whom they can give love or hate. It is only at this stage that friendships, enmities, and lasting relationships become possible.

Drs. Spock[1] and Gesell,[2] in writing about children at various ages, recognized that some premature babies develop an awareness of social behavior at a later age than their full-term counterparts, and therefore remain immature far longer. And even though children with learning differences may have been born after a full nine months, many of them also seem to mature later than their peers. The delay in their social adaptation matches their lag in learning to read and write. They progress through the expected stages, as do all children, but they always seem to be out of step with their age group. In order to understand and truly help children with learning differences, parents and teachers need to be aware that a youngster's social adjustment, or the lack of it, is part of his more general learning problems. And while most children learn socialization automatically by observation and imitation of what they see, youngsters with learning problems may have to be carefully and explicitly taught. Someday, perhaps, schools will give a course on learning how to live with others.

It is not surprising that children with learning differences have their social troubles. Many of the same deficits that affect a youngster's academic skills have implications for his social adjustment. A common trait among children with learning problems is difficulty in paying attention to what is important. They tend to become mixed up and confused in a crowded or overstimulating environment. They cannot tune out what is unimportant and tune in that which is important. This may cause them to lose the essence of a conversation or not respond appropriately. Sometimes they cannot shift gears as readily as other children. They may still be thinking about the pass they fumbled, although the gang has long since started another activity. And some youngsters' impulsivity and lack of judgment may cause them to lash out at imagined slights, turning them into poor sports.

Whether social problems begin early or late, they frequently accompany a learning disability. Many parents claim that their children's social problems are of the gravest concern—much more hurtful than the poor grades they get in school. Yet teachers and learning specialists pay very little attention to that aspect of youngsters' difficulties. In a discussion group organized for parents of children with learning differences, there was almost unanimous agreement that a child's reading problem is easier to accept than a social problem, perhaps because it is taken care of away from home. Let the school worry! Many parents in the group felt at a loss when it came to helping their children get along better with siblings and friends; moreover, there seemed to be no one they could turn to for help. After all, this was not a school problem.

Because they tend to be less mature, more impulsive, or lacking in caution, young children with potential school problems frequently cannot be permitted the freedom to play in the backyard alone at an age when most children begin exploring the neighborhood. Through no fault of their own, they have to be watched and guided more carefully. This, too, hinders their social development.

I remember Glen, who seemed particularly immature in the four-year-old class in the day-care center. He was physically, cognitively, and socially young for his age. He couldn't climb the stairs one foot at a time (expected by four), and he couldn't stand or hop on one foot. He had not learned to recognize colors or to count. He seemed frightened when his mother was not with him, so she had to remain at school long after other mothers had left their children playing happily. Years ago, it was assumed that a child who reached the ripe old age of three and a half should be able to part from his mother on the first day of nursery school, adapting easily to his teacher and new playmates. Now we know that a child's readiness to leave his mother is as individually and developmentally determined as learning to read. For Glen, it came later rather than earlier.

In school, Glen walked around hugging a stuffed dog, but he screamed in panic at a real one. He rarely played outside or participated in group activities because, as his teacher said, "Most

of the time he doesn't seem to understand what it is we're doing."
So while the children in his class sang songs, built airports with
blocks, and played house in the doll corner, Glen remained alone,
watching. The other children didn't dislike him; they just forgot
he was there. Occasionally a youngster would do something for
Glen in a protective, mothering way. It was apparent that Glen's
classmates thought of him as the baby of the class. Actually, if
Glen's parents and teachers had thought of him as one or two
years younger than his years, he probably would have seemed just
fine. He had developmental lags in learning as well as in the social
graces. It might have been preferable to keep him at home in a
more protected environment for another year. His mother could
have been his mentor and teacher until he was more prepared to
leave her and join his peers in the outside world. An arranged
meeting once or twice a week with another child his age might
have paved the way for his entering nursery school.

Joseph had language difficulties that possibly related to his
social problems in nursery school. He couldn't find the words with
which to communicate with the other children, and he tended to
strike out physically at anyone who came near. Children who
cannot express their thoughts and feelings easily become frustrated and seem to have a harder time socially. Perhaps they are
rejected because other children can't understand them. Most
young children, as well as adults, convey a multitude of thoughts
in the course of a day. They talk unselfconsciously and easily.
Only when we are forced to speak in an uncomfortable situation,
such as an oral examination, can we begin to understand the
frustration of the child with communication problems.

By the time he got to kindergarten, Joseph's language problems, his impulsivity, and his quick temper affected his interpersonal relationships as well as his academic learning. He had trouble controlling his feelings and could only express them with his
hands and feet. Children tended to avoid him rather than run the
risk of being hit or kicked, so he was alone much of the time. That
only increased his anger, and he lashed out even more. The cycle
rolled on until Joseph got into trouble in adolescence and eventu-

ally received professional treatment to help him understand and handle his feelings.

At six, Betsy was the opposite of Joseph in her approach to other children. Although she, too, had trouble both understanding verbal communication and talking to her classmates, she hugged and touched every prospective friend until he or she backed away. She made connections with people and things by feeling and touching—the way much younger children do. When she liked someone, she wanted to show it—by hugging, kissing, and grabbing. The other children in her first grade who were the objects of her affection were more able to play together and convey thoughts to each other by talking. They didn't need to touch to feel liked, and they thought Betsy was strange. Betsy, feeling the other children's dislike, became particularly possessive with one child in the class. The more she was rebuffed, the more she tried to make a friend—the wrong way.

By the time Betsy was seven, she expected to be rebuffed by her classmates and unconsciously provoked them. She used to ask "Do you like me?" at inappropriate times, inviting a negative response. She complained of mistreatment at the school-bus stop but hated the taunts of the children when her mother had to drive her to school. Eventually her claim that "Nobody likes me" seemed based more on reality than on Betsy's imagination.

Many of these lonely children do not have the faintest idea of why they are being rejected or scapegoated. They do not see their behavior as inappropriate or socially unacceptable. When asked why he thought he had no friends, one young man responded: "It's because I have allergies and my nose runs. The kids call me Sniffles." He never saw himself as the disruptive boy who constantly injected himself into other children's games and conversations, much to their annoyance. Another child in the same school made up wild stories to ingratiate herself with her classmates. She seemed surprised to learn that few, if any, believed her tales, but they did resent her "lies."

For most children, feeling smart is of utmost importance. They may say they don't care and may even stay away from those who are successful and well-liked, but deep down, they'd love to be among them. Ronny was very self-conscious about his learning problems and tended to blame his lack of friends on the fact that he couldn't read. He withdrew from social contacts in the fifth grade, hiding from the world by living behind a camera. He became a good photographer, but that didn't help his social life. He once told me why he thought he had no companions. "It's because I'm not one of the smart kids. Why they don't like me could be my reading." He really believed it—or wanted to. Actually, fourth and fifth graders love to find a scapegoat and a child's being "dumb" is as good a reason as any to choose him, particularly if the child is disturbed by teasing. And who wouldn't be!

To add to the problem, Ronny's parents were also disappointed in him. He just didn't fit into their family very well. The rest of the family was outgoing and gregarious, while Ronny was the odd man out, shy and ill at ease. Children are born with temperaments and their own personalities. They are not, as Rousseau thought many years ago, blank slates on which parents write their futures. From the beginning, some youngsters don't act in a way that parents can enjoy. It is not easy to adore a colicky or always-awake infant, or a toddler who cries too much and can't stop running long enough for a kiss. Ronny had been all this and more. His parents couldn't even have fun providing stimulating experiences for him, since he gave no indication that he was responsive to what they did. Instead, he usually became irritable in response to anything new, running around even more than usual.

Ronny rarely went to anyone's house and never invited anyone to his. His parents were concerned about his isolation and tried to push him to enter into as many activities as possible. He took music lessons, stayed for after-school sports, and attended plays and parties (to which he was invited by children of his parents' friends.) He went to all of them, whether or not he wanted to go. I remember one day when Ronny attended two performances of the same concert. His mother took him and his sister to the concert at school in the afternoon, and then he was asked to accompany a classmate's family to the evening performance. His mother wouldn't let him refuse, so Ronny went again for the second show. Needless to say, he was tired, bored, and fidgety, particularly since band concerts weren't his favorite thing.

This episode took place when Ronny was in second grade; it was already clear that his problems created both a good deal of anxiety for his parents and unhappiness for him. Ronny did not love birthday parties either. They frightened him, but he went dutifully to each and every one to which he was invited because his mother pushed him to go. She admitted that she would have been embarrassed if he refused.

In fact, many young children don't enjoy birthday parties, and the hosts may enjoy them least of all. Parties tend to be noisy and confusing, particularly for children who have trouble integrating too many impressions simultaneously. Children with learning differences can easily become overwhelmed by too much going on at the same time. They may also be afraid of playing the competitive games at a party because they never win. Birthday parties seem to have been designed for very secure, aggressive children who are always at ease and who usually win at games. I would recommend reading Chapter 5 in Judy Blume's book *Tales of a Fourth-Grade Nothing*, [3] for a nine-year-old's humorous account of his younger brother's birthday party. It tells of the disasters and traumas suffered by each of the small guests at the party. One can only conclude by the end of this hilarious description that the only person who really enjoys a three-year-old's birthday party is Mommy.

Parents of young children should attempt to understand their children's feelings and should not push them into social situations for which they are not ready. Just as we don't expect children to be comfortable skipping a grade in school, we should not expect them to rush into new social experiences. Developmental stages may be missed, creating tension and an inadequate adjustment.

However, there *are* times in the life of a family when it is important for a child to participate in a social event in which he may be challenged or ill at ease. Holidays and family gatherings are such occasions. They may be trying for parents as well as for children. A visit to relatives on Christmas Day is often fraught with tension and anxiety that seems to set everyone on edge. Countless parents have complained that a child spoiled the day for everyone by not getting along with his cousins or by bursting into tears at the least provocation. One mother told me that she expected her son to act up whenever the family visited anyone. She realized that she became tense on each and every occasion, waiting for Alex's breaking point. Perhaps because of her tension, Alex rarely disappointed her. When I asked her why she kept taking Alex to visit her relatives when it was so painful for both of them, she looked surprised and said she had never considered any alternative.

If parents have learned through experience that a child cannot manage a whole day in the company of friends, adults, or relatives, perhaps they should recognize that he would be happier staying at home with a baby sitter. The rest of the family might enjoy the outing more, too. But if a youngster does want to be with the family on such occasions, it may help to acknowledge the stress for him (and for you) and perhaps to make your visit a short one. It is better to quit while you're ahead—before things fall apart.

Parents can also make family trips easier by preparing the youngster in advance for the events of the day or week. Providing a detailed description of what might occur during the trip and packing a bag with a few of his favorite possessions to take along have prevented many a tantrum. And the useful technique of role-playing may smooth the adjustment to an unfamiliar situation by making the unexpected known and hence less threatening. For instance, if Mother acts the part of a waitress at the resort hotel and gives her child the experience of ordering his breakfast alone, it ought to make him feel more comfortable when he gets there. And when a parent takes the role of the child in a new experience, he is providing a model for him to emulate.

For many youngsters, too much of a good thing can be worse than none at all. A disappointed mother described what should have been an ideal day for the family. In celebration of Rob and his twin sister's birthday, the family spent the day in the city, doing all the things both children loved. After lunch at the automat, they went to the zoo, which was Rob's choice. Next were ice cream and a trip to their father's office, followed by a family dinner in Chinatown.

As Rob's mother reported, all was well until after the ice cream. Suddenly, upon arriving at the office, Rob had an unexplained temper tantrum and just fell apart. The restaurant was a nightmare, too, with Rob running all around and not eating. No one could understand what had happened. The day had started out so well, and Rob had seemed so happy.

In retrospect, it was easy to see what had occurred. The perfectly planned day should have been divided into two or even three exciting days. The plans were just too ambitious for Rob. He was reacting as any child would who had been exposed to too much stress—only Rob's boiling point was quite a few degrees lower than his sister's.

A child's social intelligence has little to do with IQ. One of the boys I'll always remember was Steve. I met him when he was in first grade. He was probably the most brilliant boy who ever came into my office. He broke all records on IQ tests, but at first had great difficulty learning to read and write. He had even greater problems with friends. He was clumsy in his movements, and as he grew, he was never welcomed on the athletic field. He seemed to know that he'd probably drop the ball or make the first out, so he usually just watched on the sidelines, yelling curse words at anyone who made an error. Perhaps it made him feel better to tell someone else how bad he was, but it hardly ingratiated him with the other boys.

Once in a while Steve tried to have other children come to play at his house after school. He wanted to have friends, but he couldn't share his possessions easily and simply had to have his own way. It was a matter of "do it my way or not at all." Shortly after a new friend arrived to play, there would be tears and the boy would go home, never to be seen again. Steve was devastated. He never knew what had happened. He couldn't see how his own actions offended others because his own needs got in the way.

Occasionally, Steve's father would try to tell him that he was being too bossy and a poor sport with his friends. However, as was to be expected, this only led to further anguish. Steve couldn't help himself, and his father's criticism seemed unfair. One of the ways Steve's parents eventually helped him entertain his friends at home was to be on hand to supervise the children's activities fairly closely. It is certainly desirable for youngsters to handle their own social arrangements and for parents to be uninvolved, but sometimes children are not ready to take over. A planned short walk to the ice cream store or the local five-and-dime, followed by a ride home on the bus or by car, might be as much of a social engagement as a young child can manage. The next time the children get together, the parents may be able to disappear for a few minutes. Remember that a pleasant short visit is worth many longer failures.

Steve became an outstanding student in school long before he mastered the social graces. He remained a loner for several years, only occasionally interacting with boys and girls of his own age. His inability to compete in athletics, his poor self-control, and his need to be the boss made him less than appealing as a friend. Eventually, though, he became the best mathematician in his grade, and that gave him a certain status. He tutored younger children, and through them began to glean some insight into his own behavior.

While Steve probably won't ever be a Mr. Gregarious, he has learned to be more tactful in his dealings with people. And there is a happy ending. He now attends an out-of-town college where he has found a level of friendship meaningful to him. One of the nice things about being an adult is that it is possible to avoid athletics if one chooses and to concentrate instead on one's own areas of strength without appearing strange.

It's not that Steve or boys like him don't care about being accepted by their peers. Quite the contrary, most youngsters of school age want desperately to belong, but for many children with learning differences, the nature of their disorder seems to drive away the very people who mean the most to them. They may be like any of the children described thus far—perhaps immature or shy, overly aggressive or bossy, selfish or tactless. Their attitudes and behavior make them appear different, somewhat out of step with their peer group. And much more than other children, youngsters with learning problems tend to be ingenuous, naive, even gullible. This gullibility makes these youngsters particularly vulnerable to innumerable hurts and humiliations. In this age of precocious and sophisticated children, gullibility is the quality most misunderstood by others. It would be easier for many young-sters if they truly did not care about having friends. But they usually want so much to belong that they are willing to believe and trust everyone. In addition, their lack of wide social experi-ence leaves them without the ability to discriminate wisely.

Most of us anticipate social situations and quickly and accu-rately interpret people's reactions to us. We know all too well when someone is displeased, even though he may be talking softly and his words are not harsh. Body language or other nonverbal communication gives us essential clues as to how people feel. Many learning-disabled children have difficulty perceiving the subtleties of social interaction. They fail both to observe facial and body gestures and to know the meaning of a touch; the tone of a voice eludes them.

Lacking the ability to zero in and read those signals, chil-dren with learning differences misinterpret humor as well as anger and may be at a loss as to how to respond to others. Upon running into a neighbor who casually asks, "How are you?" they may tell him more than he wants to know—in great detail. An-other child might chatter gaily on about his dog's newest trick, insensitive to the fact that his neighbor's dog has just died. One young man innocently called loudly across the aisle on a bus: "Mom, why is that man so wrinkled?" We can accept this from a four-year-old, but it seems inappropriate and insulting when the speaker is ten.

"He's clumsy and I don't mean physically." That is how one mother described her ten-year-old son's social behavior. It seems an apt description for many of the children who constantly em-barrass their siblings and parents with inappropriate actions and remarks.

· "He tells the neighbors about each fight my husband and I have."

- "We can't discuss anything personal at dinner any more because he will find someone to tell."

- "He doesn't know when to stop and let people leave. He seems to want to hang onto people, even on the telephone."

- "He always says the wrong thing at the wrong time. He didn't have to tell his uncle that I said he was lazy and irresponsible."

For many children with learning differences, their inappropriate behavior reflects their prolonged egocentricity and their lack of sensitivity to others. They simply don't know how others feel nor how they themselves appear to others. They only know that they have very few friends, no one seems to understand them, and they have no idea why. On the other hand, some youngsters seem particularly tuned in to what's going on around them. They seem to know intuitively when to leave a friend alone and when not to crack a joke. I've heard the expression "street-wise" used to describe this kind of ability. Reading may be hard for them, but these youngsters know how to read people. It's a great trait to have!

It can be lonely when one is without a friend. As a consequence, some children ally themselves with the losers in their class or in the neighborhood—anyone who will like them and respond to their offer of friendship. A pecking order exists for choosing one's friends, even as in the animal kingdom. We tend to select people who are like us in some way or who mirror what we are, or think we are. But for some youngsters, it may come down to a matter of who is left to choose. They may start at the top and go down the social ladder until they can find someone with whom they can relate. For Michael, in third grade, it was a new boy from Sweden who couldn't speak a word of English. The others in the neighborhood were appropriately helpful to Sven, but Michael tried to devour him. It was great to have a constant companion who padded along behind you and never talked back. Once Sven learned English, though, he joined the other guys on the ball field, and that was the end of another friendship for Michael.

Parents may complain that their son or daughter is going with the "worst child in the class, a terrible influence." They will mention the undesirable language and the mischief the youngsters get into together. Though their child may simply enjoy the mischief, it may well be that his choice of a friend is the result of having no choice. A child's selection of a pal usually reflects some admiration for him—unless he is the only one in the neighborhood with whom he can feel comfortable. The other kids may seem "too smart" or "too snobby."

Parents will undoubtedly find it difficult to watch a relationship in which their child is the underdog being led down the proverbial garden path, but this friendship may be a first step in the child's learning to handle a social interaction. With understanding and patience, he will be able to go on to bigger and better friendships when he is more secure. In the meantime, he needs your help and support. Too often parents try to minimize the pain that a child feels by saying, "It's really nothing. You'll find another friend." A child needs to know that a parent will understand and accept his pain without crumbling under the impact or pushing him away. Home must be a bulwark of strength when a child is feeling weak. A simple "I know how much this must hurt" will help him live through a rejection or assault.

As I've said, some children with learning differences observe less in their environment, misperceive more, and may not learn as easily from experience as their friends do. And because of their immaturity and social clumsiness, they may be excluded by peers. However, like all children, they want acceptance, but their eagerness may cause them to try too hard in inappropriate ways. As a result, their social experiences become even more limited, giving them fewer opportunities to learn how to act with others. Parents, teachers, and neighbors should try to teach them the social nuances. These children *can* learn, but they may have to be taught many of the social responses that other youngsters pick up unconsciously.

An important aspect of a child's social adjustment is his skill in playing games. Most children of nine or ten know a dozen or more card games and every board game from Monopoly to Mastermind. However, many children have trouble learning and remembering the rules of a game and feel as inept in that arena as they do in the classroom. A child who has difficulty remembering the days of the week will find it hard to recall the steps of a game. In addition, it is hard for some children with learning differences to wait their turn. Their much-discussed impulsivity and their need to win get in the way. They may even tell you they hate games. It takes patience to finish most games, and their interest wanes quickly, particularly when they're losing.

I spend a fair amount of time in my office teaching youngsters how to play games. Such time is well spent, for game-playing accomplishes many things. First, children master the rules and the directions in sequence. Games also provide a social learning experience for children. They learn to share, to take turns, to trust their opponent, and eventually even to lose without a tantrum. As one child said, "I don't care if I win. I just hate to lose." Most of us do! Not surprisingly, though, most children with learning problems feel that they lose all the time. Perhaps they do—in more than just games.

One young boy always wanted to play the card game War, the only game he had played successfully. But he usually forgot the name of the game and even how to play. "I know how, but I forget," was his way of asking me to tell him again. It took many weeks for him to master that one game, but it was worth it. Among other things, it provided him with something to do when his brother deigned to play with him on a rainy day. Frequently a child will want to play the same game over and over until his parents and siblings are sick of it and wonder why he isn't too. This may reflect his need to master a skill that doesn't come easily or the wish to feel good about something he's doing. It may take him a long time to learn another game.

On sunny days, most parents have but a single thought for their children's spare time: "Go play outside." For some youngsters, this is the command they dread the most. They can't go out on the playground because no one will play with them—even though there may be an apartment house full of children under the age of ten. They claim the other boys won't let them in their games, and they usually return home a half-hour later in tears, only to be sent out again by their distraught and frustrated parents.

For Mike, almost nine, this was a typical scene, one that happened week after week. He was rejected by the kids on the block but was sent out to battle again and again by his parents, who couldn't stand to see him alone in front of the TV set day after day. Finally, after many bruises, physical and otherwise, Mike did find a group of younger children to play with. He liked kickball better than baseball anyway and at times even felt like a leader. The fact that the other boys were only six didn't bother Mike, but it was of concern to his parents. This was one problem they hadn't bargained for. They could accept the fact that Mike couldn't read well, but playing outside had nothing to do with that. They told him in no uncertain terms that he should play with boys more his own age, and then they called me for confirmation. While I could understand their concern, I felt it was important for Mike's parents to acknowledge that he *was* both less mature emotionally than the boys his age and not as adept in sports. Under the circumstances, it seemed better for him to associate with the younger children with whom he felt comfortable than to sit alone or rely on his parents for companionship. Practicing his social skills on the six-year-olds might eventually lead to more appropriate relationships.

Johnny used to stand alone on the school playground, sucking on one finger and twisting a lock of hair. Most of the sixth graders were too engrossed in the game to even notice that Johnny wasn't playing with them, but he wouldn't have been missed anyway. And most of the time, Johnny wasn't even watching. He was standing too far away—where no one could see the occasional tear in his eye.

Johnny rarely participated in any of the games at school. He didn't like being the last one chosen by the captain for the day, and as he put it, "If you don't play, you can't lose." He confessed, though, that since there was no one to be with during recess and there was nothing to do, he hated recess even more than reading or math. It was the loneliest time of the school day for him.

Inside the classroom, Johnny had his own ways of getting even. Almost without realizing it, he used to annoy the other children. He pushed pencils off their desks, disturbed them when they were trying to work, and generally made a nuisance of himself. He complained that the other children bothered *him*, but he didn't seem to be aware that he played an active role in the teasing. He only knew that he was not happy in school, and given a choice, would much prefer to stay home. And in fact, when Johnny didn't have to go to school in the summer, he did much better. He went to a day camp for children with learning problems, where he was very happy. He made new friends on the bus and received glowing reports from his counselors.

While summer vacations can be a great relief for many children, they frequently pose problems for their parents. I am often asked for advice on what a learning-disabled youngster should do in the summer. Should he stay home and be tutored in hopes of closing the educational gap, should he go away to camp for the social experience, or should he just relax at home? It all depends. If the pressure on him has been great during the school year, perhaps a relaxing summer at home without more schoolwork would be best, particularly if there are other children with whom to play. I knew a twelve-year-old who spent the summer painting a basement floor—and loved every minute of it. But if a youngster has trouble organizing his time or would spend the summer lying on his bed watching TV, he obviously needs direction. In such a case, a community recreation program or camp might be important. (Some even have remediation as part of the program.) For older youngsters, a camp away from home can foster independence and improve social adaptability as well as athletic skills. Since camps are expensive, though, the decision ought to be made with a great deal of thought.

The choice of camp again depends on the development and needs of the camper. If a boy or girl has a poor tolerance for new situations and is anxious about leaving home, the protective environment of a special camp close by might be best. In general, a highly competitive camp situation imposes the same stress on the youngster that he has had during the school year and should be avoided, unless of course he is a star athlete. If a child goes to a regular camp or into a regular recreation program, parents should be honest with the director about any unique problems or special needs their child has.

Summertime can provide a good opportunity for a child to indulge in what he needs most. For one youngster, it might mean tutoring two or three times weekly to prevent a backslide in newly gained reading skills; for another, it might be going to a hiking or fishing camp in the wilds of Maine, while for yet another child, it might be going to the community swimming pool with his family, whenever the spirit moves them. Discussing possible alternatives with a child's teacher, learning specialist, or physician should help to clarify the priorities for a family.

For many boys and girls with learning differences (and perhaps without, as well), their social problems are possibly the saddest part of their lives and perhaps the most difficult to remediate. Most of the suggestions that I can give to parents are merely Band-aids, not cures. Only a parent's understanding and patient support can help a child learn to live with others and handle the frustration in the interim. And this isn't easy, because a parent's feelings are aroused too. Memories of one's own hurts and unfulfilled childhood wishes make it especially hard to be objective. However, there are a few rules of thumb that might help the communication between parent and child during difficult times.

1. When he tells you his troubles, don't blame him or say they don't exist. Acknowledge his pain and try to help him with the realities. Empathy, not judgment, may be all he is asking for.

2. "How could you go about making Jimmy your friend?" is a valid question to ask a boy or girl. Sometimes getting youngsters to look head-on at the requirements for a successful relationship may give them new insight.

3. Bribery might get you everywhere. Promising a reward for a successful, lasting date with another child might encourage him to exercise that extra bit of control.

4. Talking about controls can be effective. A parent can acknowledge that a child might find it hard to restrain himself, but that as he grows, it is expected. Setting standards for behavior (as discussed in Chapter 3) is important.

5. Patience on the part of parents helps too. The recognition that children who are less mature than their peers may take longer to become ready for socialization may relieve the pressure for both parent and child. Just as some people are not ready for marriage and a family at twenty, some boys and girls are not able to handle a sleep-over at eight or nine. It might help to remember that most youngsters don't become reclusive adults, but eventually do find relationships that are comfortable and right for them.

Parents and teachers are usually more aware of children's social difficulties when they are in elementary school than when they are older. Younger children tend to be more open about their troubles, revealing their slights and hurts more readily. As they grow into the middle years, they become more self-protective and secretive. Also, teachers in junior and senior high school usually see too many students in the course of a day to really get to know any of them well. It is the rare teacher who becomes a mentor for a teenager, particularly since teachers' primary concerns are with the academic subjects they teach. So it is possible for the lonely youngster in middle school to be suffering in silence, making it hard for others to comprehend why his behavior seems so antisocial.

Sometimes parents or teachers sense a youngster's isolation from the group, but they are powerless to do much about it. Most budding adolescents would not take kindly to planned and guided social activities. They resent parental interference, even when it is well meant. At this time most boys and girls begin to cut the ties at home, and the peer group takes over as all-important. Youngsters at this stage want most to conform and be like everyone else, even to the holes in the jeans and the sneakers that are in vogue at the moment. But youngsters with learning problems often appear different, perhaps even more so than when they were younger. Their handicaps seem more visible to others and more all-encompassing. They may talk too much, too loudly, and too repetitively. Their continuing immaturity and weaker sense of identity make it harder for them to do what is expected, and their lack of a backlog of social experiences leaves them with a less than adequate repertoire of behaviors to use when the chips are down. If they can't stay cool under fire and have no staunch friend to come to their defense, scapegoating can be particularly vicious. Even without problems, most adolescents feel unsure of themselves and are only too willing to exalt themselves by tearing down weaker peers. The youngster with a handicap becomes a perfect foil.

At this stage in life, too, boys and girls become more discriminating and selective about who may become part of their social world. They derive a sense of status from those with whom they associate. Unfortunately, the learning-disabled youngster is often regarded as a low-status person, and therefore to be avoided —all the more reason for the adults in his world to help him develop his area of greatest competence. If he is a good soccer player, he will make the team, and if he is an artist, he will be asked to draw posters for school elections. This will help others to see him not primarily as learning disabled, but as someone with something to offer.

Jerry, a member of a minority group in a predominantly white community, was on the fringes of a rather rowdy group of eighth-grade boys. He didn't actually start the fights or break the windows, but he was an observer to these events and the activists were his friends. Jerry had a long history of academic problems in school, but it was only in the middle school that he began to seek the excitement and the notoriety that this group offered. A boy or girl who may be afraid to compete in the world of achievers may find it easier to be the "bad guy."

Luckily Jerry was a good soccer player who made the school team. He stayed for practice every day after school and gained recognition for his prowess. However, when his marks were poor or if he and his friends got into any trouble, Jerry's parents threatened to keep him from playing soccer. It was not hard for me to convince them, though, that this was probably the single most important activity for him and should not be used as punishment. Not only did playing soccer keep him busy after school (and out of trouble), but it gave him status—in a positive way.

Youngsters whose peers reject or attack them can express their pain through a range of negative behaviors—beginning with rowdiness and ending with delinquency. Psychological literature is beginning to report the links and connections between undiagnosed and unremediated learning differences and later delinquency. It is easy today for boys and girls to get into trouble. They are given more freedom to roam and have less responsibility at home than children did a generation ago. As a result, a youngster who needs to find acceptance might, like Jerry, go along with the gang, suffering the consequences of its actions, preferring negative attention to none at all.

Craig, mild-mannered and conforming throughout elementary school, had an inordinate need to be part of the group. The only way the eighth-grade boys would accept him was if he did their dirty work. If a pack of cigarettes was to be copped from the local store, Craig was selected to do the job. He had two strikes against him from the beginning: he allowed himself to be exploited; and because of his lack of social sophistication, he usually was caught red-handed, while the other boys walked away innocently.

There is little doubt that life is easier for a teenager if he has even one good friend to help him feel important and needed. But to become a true friend means to be caring and sensitive to another's needs and feelings. The required give-and-take is often hard for the adolescent with a learning difference. If he lacks an adequate sense of who he is and is still egocentric, his friendships may be like one-way streets. He will be unable to share much of himself with another, but will tend to use the other to fulfill his own self-centered needs. For many young adults, getting past their own immaturity and their self-concerns can be a major stumbling block in developing good mutual relationships with members of the same or of the opposite sex.

Parents frequently ask whether their adolescents with learning differences should associate with other teenagers with problems or seek recreation among the general population of their peers. As might be expected, there is no pat answer. It depends on the individual and the extent of his problems. If he is very shy, behaves inappropriately in a social gathering, and has few, if any, friends, a supervised group of other learning-disabled youngsters might be necessary to fill the gap. On the other hand, if he can manage in the mainstream, even with help, surely that should be encouraged.

I'm reminded of Sara, who struggled with a lisp as well as a learning difference all through school. With sheer determination not to appear different, she achieved amazing results. She refused to take slower courses in the high school and made an equally strong effort to make friends. By the eleventh grade, her grades were good and she had a boyfriend. She had also developed much of the social savvy that had been so obviously missing when she was younger.

Sara was the first to admit that life had not been easy for her. She told of studying very hard and of going to the math center almost daily throughout the year for extra help when she would have preferred to meet her boyfriend and the gang for a soda. However, she took great pride in her success in both areas. Only her SAT scores, the lowest in the school, reflected the extent of her learning problems.

Can parents help at all? I am often asked whether it is too late for parents to make a difference in their teenagers' attitudes and social adjustment. Far from being too late, I think parents have a second chance at this time to rebuild and restructure relationships with their children, who in this transitional period are building bridges between childhood and adulthood. Communication can be a significant part of that bridge. The following are a few suggestions for parents, to help their adolescents with learning and social problems.

1. Encourage good self-care. An adolescent may remember to patch his blue jeans but not to brush his teeth or use a deodor-

ant. Bodily changes are rapid, and personal hygiene is particularly important through these years. Unobtrusive reminders are not intended to embarrass a youngster but to enhance his image with others.

2. Peer conformity is all important at this stage. Try not to insist on a short haircut or button-down shirt if ponytails and work shirts are in. Your child needs to feel part of the peer group. This may be an artificial way to join them, but join them he will. Save your confrontations for the more important issues.

3. Guide your youngster in just plain everyday good manners and appropriate conversation. Devise a system of subtle clues that only he will recognize to teach him not to interrupt conversations and to modulate his voice as well as his repetitive comments. It is well worth the effort and should contribute to his acceptability in public.

4. Teach him that he cannot always have instant gratification. At times he may have to postpone getting what he wants or find an alternative. If you are busy and cannot drive him to his friend's, he may have to find another means of transportation or wait until you are available. This is a good time to begin to change some of the less desirable behavior patterns that have persisted too long.

5. No teenager can afford to be ignorant about sex in these liberated times. Yet he may not understand his sexual urges or his fantasies if he has not learned what to expect through social experience and talk sessions. A clear, forthright discussion may clear up some misconceptions and diminish his guilt. Remember, his curiosity and his fantasies are normal. He may just be too tied up with his own uncertainties to feel free to explore the mysteries of sex, even in books.

6. Teach him how to be comfortable with the activities that precede dating. Walking a girl home, talking on the telephone, or going to a boy-girl party may seem overwhelming to him. He may need very specific instructions on how to act.

7. Help your adolescent find an appropriate group to join. He may be devastated when he cannot get in with the jocks at school, but there may be a group of local fishermen who would welcome him aboard. Church groups, Y clubs, theater groups, or tennis clinics may provide a place for him to meet peers. But an adolescent's individuality must be respected, and parents cannot let their own social values impinge on his. Some youngsters at this age truly don't want or are not ready for an active social life. If he is not morose, so be it.

8. Help and encourage a teenager to become independent. This means teaching him (and allowing him) to travel and shop for clothing alone, as well as to be aware of his own goals. As an adult, he will not be able to rely on parents for decisions, so he might as well begin now. The choice of ski pants or books to read should be his, wherever possible. Wearing a sweater because your mother is cold, as many children do, is no longer appropriate.

If nothing seems to work and you continue to be concerned about signs of trouble with your adolescent, seek professional help. Today, there is little if any stigma attached to seeing a therapist or counselor, and it may prevent future problems. The social aspects of a child's life are too important to ignore. Parents need to take a long-range view of youngsters' social lives and plan their helping strategies as carefully as they do their children's education. If we neglect to teach our offspring social skills, all the academic teaching in the world won't prepare them for adulthood.

Chapter 5

Life at School

When the school census taker came around counting prospective students for the new school being built, Mrs. Brown laughed. Her only child, Teddy, was ten months old, and the thought of school was remote. Yet it seemed only a minute later that she held him by the hand as they entered that large brick building with the scrubbed desks and polished floors. It was a morning in early September, and Teddy was trying to act very grown up. He let go of his mother's hand and went into the school. But what should have been his first successful experience away from home became a nightmare within the first few months. In retrospect, Teddy's parents said that Teddy had seemed a very different—and happier—child before he started school.

As an infant, nothing in Teddy's development had seemed particularly unusual. A happy, cheerful baby, he walked and talked when the other children in the neighborhood did. But all this changed in the first few months of school. What had happened to cause his bad moods, his frequent nightmares, and his complaints about school? Although no one recognized or diagnosed his problems at the beginning, we now know that Teddy had a learning disability involving almost all modalities.

Let's follow him for the next several years to see what children with learning differences may experience as they go through school and what their parents may have to deal with in the course of their children's education.

Early in his kindergarten experience, when Teddy came home cranky from school, his mother was sympathetic but unconcerned. She thought he was irritable because of the new group of children and the long morning. Mrs. Brown assumed that Teddy would settle down in time. But when Teddy kept complaining about his "mean teacher" and the "hard work," she became more concerned. When he reverted to wetting his bed at night, she thought of going to school to talk to his teacher but felt uncomfortable about doing so. Maybe Teddy's teacher would think that she was blaming her or that she was, at the very least, an overanxious mother.

Many parents, particularly of first children, are, like Teddy's mother, reluctant to discuss a youngster's problems with school personnel. They conform to an imagined rule of protocol: "Don't call us, we'll call you"—and that usually happens only when disciplinary measures are called for. Most adults of today grew up in awe of anyone in the role of pedagogue. When these adults were young, the school and its teachers represented authority; such a firmly entrenched image is not easily discarded. So they stay away from the school and let the teachers educate their children.

That's fine for the children who adapt easily to school and have no difficulty learning. But sometimes parents must put aside their fear of going to school and take a more assertive stand for their children's sake, particularly when a youngster is having difficulty adjusting to school. A child with school problems may well need an advocate, someone who can run interference for him. After all, he spends most of his day in school, and that is where he is most vulnerable.

Parents and teachers are both involved in the daily life of a child, and most teachers today welcome as much information from home as they can get. In all probability, Teddy's teacher would have wanted very much to know right away that Teddy was so unhappy about school.

Finally, in November, Teddy's teacher called Mrs. Brown, asking that she come to school for a conference. His teacher realized that something was wrong. Most of Teddy's behaviors would have been perfectly acceptable in a nursery school class, which is one of the reasons his teacher didn't spot his learning difference right away. She merely saw him as young for his age and not ready for formal learning.

Her heart pounding, Mrs. Brown went to school. The conference went something like this: "Teddy's a darling little boy, but he seems quite immature for kindergarten. It is hard for him to sit still, and he wanders aimlessly around the room much of the morning. He can't seem to focus on a group activity, even briefly, and he is very easily distracted. Some of the children in the class are learning to read, but Teddy doesn't recognize many of the letters or numbers and won't let me try to teach him. He still can't write his name and says he doesn't want to learn. But he's a *delight* to have in the class!" (Teachers often make this last mollifying comment in a sincere attempt to add a positive note.)

For the next fifteen minutes, Teddy's teacher and Mrs. Brown talked about what Mrs. Brown might do at home to help Teddy and what his teacher could do to help him to be more comfortable in school. Teddy had once confided to his mother that "I need to sit on my teacher's lap more." The teacher suggested that Mrs. Brown read to Teddy at home, count objects around the house, and put a few magnetic letters on the refrigerator door for Teddy to recognize.

Mrs. Brown had mixed emotions when she left the school, but she was glad she had talked to Teddy's teacher. His teacher had seemed to know Teddy, after all, and to understand the reasons for his unhappiness at school. Mrs. Brown was not as worried about Teddy now, feeling confident that she could help him learn his letters at home, away from the distractions of the noisy classroom. At the same time, she felt somewhat remiss in not having taught Teddy letters and numbers earlier, as the other mothers undoubtedly had. But she had thought she might confuse him by teaching him differently; besides, that was what he was going to school for. Mrs. Brown also admitted to herself that Teddy hadn't seemed the slightest bit interested in the books she had tried to read to him, and he couldn't seem to remember the names of colors or numbers even after they had been repeated to him many times.

When Mrs. Brown tried to work with Teddy at home, he was very resistant. He said he didn't like *work*, which meant anything that he had to sit down for or pay attention to, and he usually refused outright to have anything to do with letters and numbers. The teaching sessions at home quickly deteriorated into temper tantrums and tears, and little was accomplished. It was not a happy time for Teddy or his parents. He soon developed a full-fledged dislike of school.

In the spring, Teddy's teacher and the principal suggested to the Browns that perhaps Teddy should repeat kindergarten the next year. He didn't seem ready for the work of first grade, and another year in kindergarten might give him a chance to "grow up." While Mr. and Mrs. Brown were not completely surprised to hear the recommendation that Teddy stay back, they didn't like the idea. They remembered that when they were in school only the "dummies" had been kept back and were teased unmercifully. Some of their parents, who had been embarrassed, too, had even said that their children had been "sick for a year." Besides, what would their friends and Teddy's grandparents say? The Browns lived in a community in which everyone would know. The stigma seemed more than they could handle.

Teddy's parents also thought that maybe the school was judging Teddy prematurely. Perhaps he would mature over the summer. And even if he didn't, there was always time later on to consider his repeating a grade. Wherever possible, schools usually try to honor parents' feelings in matters such as retention, so it was decided to let Teddy move on with his classmates to the first grade in the fall.

Whether or not to retain a child in a grade is never easy to decide—for the parents or the school. A child's growth and development aren't entirely predictable, and one must always weigh the benefits against the obvious disadvantages. Staying back can be a blow to a child's ego and other children *may* ridicule him. Some schools today have a policy never to retain a child, while others use retention frequently for children who don't seem ready for the work of the next grade. This policy varies from district to district.

If the school does recommend retention for your child, you should consider several factors. Most important, of course, is what the child stands to gain from it. If a youngster seems capable but immature in many areas—social, academic, and emotional—an additional year might well give him a chance to consolidate his skills and do the necessary growing. It also gives the capable child an opportunity for leadership that he would otherwise lack. Many parents these days are even asking nursery schools to keep a child for an extra year, particularly if that child is a boy with a birthday late in the year. In general, during their young years boys seem less mature than girls and are perhaps less ready to adapt to the routine of school.

To justify retaining a youngster in a grade higher than kindergarten or first grade, one should be able to predict that the child would be consistently performing at least in the middle—or better yet, near the top—of the class by the next year. If, on the other hand, it seems that he will still be on the bottom in academic skills, I would seriously question the advisability of such a move. Then other measures such as careful diagnosis or educational therapy are called for. For many youngsters with learning differences, therefore, holding them back is not the answer. Many are much more than one year behind their classmates and they learn slowly. If retained, they would still be at the lower end of the class, with no boost to their egos and few academic advantages.

School officials frequently suggest retention for a child with poor reading skills or a weakness in one academic subject. This was the reason that retention was recommended for Daniel, a first grader in Teddy's school. (Unlike Teddy, he had seemed fine in kindergarten.) Daniel was a very bright, attractive child who couldn't read, it was true, but who excelled in arithmetic. He was also a leader among his classmates. He was verbal and imaginative, and his artistic talent and fund of knowledge were amazing.

Daniel's parents didn't know what to do about Daniel's staying in first grade for another year and they asked my advice. I was glad they had. Although I don't often disagree with the opinion of school personnel, I felt that retention would have been wrong for Daniel. He was participating in every activity in the class, except reading, and he seemed to be learning and contributing. I felt it was important for him to continue to learn through every means possible until he could begin to read. Reading is not all a child learns in school. It is an important skill, to be sure, but children can also learn by living and listening. Daniel would have fit into next year's first grade *only* in reading. In every other way, he would have been out of step. For retention to be successful, the *whole* child has to benefit from the additional year.

And finally, for retention to be effective, there must be acceptance on the part of the parents. This doesn't mean just verbal acknowledgment that retention is a good idea. It means that parents can honestly support their child's spending another year in a grade. Only then can they help the youngster understand the reasons for it and withstand the possible criticism and teasing of friends and neighbors.

I know of one family whose three sons all repeated first grade very successfully, the youngest at the request of his parents. Two of the boys had November birthdays and were therefore young for the class, and the third son just seemed immature. None of the boys had a particularly difficult time accepting the retention. It became the accepted thing to do in their family, and all the children appeared to benefit significantly. The two older boys, who had not learned to read in first grade, went on to become superior students. Perhaps they would have anyway but with much more stress in the early years.

On the other hand, when parents cannot accept the idea of retention, it cannot be as successful and should not be forced. Of course, school personnel should make every effort to help parents support the idea, and this may take several weeks or months, but if in the end parents cannot come to terms with it, retention may be detrimental to the child.

To sum up, repetition of a grade may be helpful when a child seems bright, but young, and not prepared for many aspects of the next grade. Usually, the earlier retention takes place in a child's schooling, the easier it will be for him—but only if his parents support the idea. Conversely, repetition of a grade is not recommended if the child will continue to be at the bottom of the class or will soon lag behind again because of learning problems. And it doesn't seem advisable to hold a child back when he is deficient in only one area of learning, such as reading. There is more to learning than just reading and writing. His social life at school is also important, and if he is going to be the "granddaddy" of the class, another look should be taken at how he might benefit from that role.

But let's return to Teddy's story. He did not repeat kindergarten but entered first grade. His parents waited anxiously to see what this year would bring. They didn't say anything to Teddy's new teacher about his problems in kindergarten, hoping against hope that maybe Teddy's teacher of last year hadn't brought out the best in him. They also felt they might give the first-grade teacher food for thought, so to speak, if they told her about Teddy's difficulties. Perhaps he merely got off to a slow start and this year would be better.

At first Teddy went off to school each morning without complaint and brought home papers stamped with a "smile face." But soon that changed too. He began to dawdle on school mornings, occasionally asking if he could stay home from school because he had a stomach ache. He frequently told his father he wished there were no such thing as school. It soon became apparent that things weren't going so well this year either. And on the days when a substitute teacher ran the class, he often came home in tears. He spoke of having been made to read aloud—when he couldn't—and shamed in front of the class. Once the whole class was kept in from recess while Teddy finished copying his sentence from the board.

One day in December, the school psychologist called Mrs. Brown, asking for permission to test Teddy. His teacher had made the referral because Teddy didn't seem to be making much progress in reading and seemed so unhappy in school. The psychologist explained that he would try to determine, in the course of his evaluation, what was wrong.

Six weeks later, the Browns went to school to learn the results of the psychologist's evaluation. He said that Teddy was of average intelligence but that he probably had a specific learning disability which was making it hard for him to learn to read and write. Teddy was also quite distractible and was finding it very difficult to learn in the casual atmosphere of his classroom.

Teddy had been carefully placed in an open classroom, where there is less structure in the daily schedule than in a traditional self-contained class. In an open classroom, children may even select their own activities and lessons—up to a point—and they are free to move about the classroom during the day. Youngsters are not expected to remain seated at assigned desks, but may choose to work in the reading corner, at the science center, or at the math table, designated areas within the class. It was felt that Teddy could learn at his own pace in this kind of class and not feel so far behind his classmates, since there were few group activities.

However, after testing Teddy, the psychologist felt that the choice of class had been inappropriate. The extra movement and distraction in the room seemed to bother Teddy. He never knew just where he should be or what he ought to be doing. No wonder Teddy was frustrated in school!

Rather than change Teddy's class at this point in the year, though, the psychologist suggested that his teacher try to structure Teddy's day and supervise him more closely. Henceforth, when Teddy came to school in the morning, waiting for him would be a contract outlining the work he should accomplish during the day. His teacher would also help Teddy move from one learning area of the room to another, since this seemed a problem for him. He often got "lost" en route, taking frequent walks down the hall to the bathroom.

The psychologist told the Browns more about Teddy's problems in learning. For the first time, they began to understand why Teddy couldn't concentrate on his work and why he seemed to forget things so easily. Then the psychologist said that perhaps Teddy would eventually need a special class in order to get the extra help he needed. Although no decision would be made until the end of the year, it might be a good idea for the Browns to see the special classes for children with learning disabilities in the area. However, the psychologist assured Mr. and Mrs. Brown,

Teddy should definitely stay where he was, at least for the rest of the year. The school had the resources to help him, now that his learning problems were recognized.

The next week, Teddy began going to the resource room in his school for forty minutes every day. There he worked with a learning disabilities teacher, either alone or in a small group of two or three children, on skills in which he was weak.

A resource room is only one of the possible facilities within a school designed to help youngsters with learning differences and other handicaps. Children are referred there for specific help in behavioral or educational skills, with grouping usually based on educational needs. A resource teacher trained in learning disabilities provides direct and indirect services to children. The direct service is the individual teaching given to the youngsters who come to the resource room, learning center, or helping place (as they are sometimes called) for a specified time daily or several times weekly. This arrangement allows the children to be "mainstreamed" in regular classes for most of the day.

Resource-room teachers can also—as an indirect service—consult with classroom teachers, giving suggestions to help the children for whom learning is difficult. In some schools, the resource room is also available on a flexible basis to any student who feels he needs temporary help or additional support with schoolwork.

For Teddy, the resource room was a haven. He felt secure there, knowing that the other children were in the same boat. It was the one place in school he didn't feel like a failure. In fact, he usually got 100 percent on his papers. For Teddy, the resource room was a respite from the pressures of the classroom. Although some of his classmates objected to going there for help, it was really his saving grace that year. His teacher helped him in the classroom too. Among other things, she cut the required spelling list for the week and carefully planned the work contract for Teddy to do each day. She knew what his learning needs were and scheduled his work accordingly.

Teddy's teacher made other accommodations, too. She knew that Teddy's attention span was short and that he couldn't stay with a task for a long time. She made a deal with him. When he felt he had to move around, he could leave the room to get a drink at the water fountain, but only if he came right back. Teddy enjoyed this responsibility and usually didn't abuse the privilege. As with most youngsters with learning problems, most of Teddy's needs were handled within the classroom by his regular teacher, supplemented by the special services available in the school.

By April, Teddy had begun to read a little and didn't seem quite so unhappy in school. He had made a few friends in the class, and they included him in the games at recess. When the Browns met with Teddy's classroom teacher, resource teacher, school psychologist, and the principal in May, the consensus was that Teddy should continue in a regular class next year—though in a more traditional classroom setting. The school would continue to provide special resource help for Teddy.

In September, at the very beginning of second grade, Teddy's parents went to school to meet with Teddy's new teacher. They told her all about what Teddy could and couldn't do, and how he showed his frustration with learning by resisting work and withdrawing. It was decided at this meeting that the school would provide frequent progress reports and that neither Teddy's teacher nor his parents would wait until small problems became big ones to communicate with each other. Teddy's parents also asked that the teacher read the psychologist's report from the previous year as well as the comments from the resource teacher.

The beginning of each year is the right time for parents of a child with a learning difference to make contact with a classroom teacher. Parents are sometimes reluctant to tell teachers about a youngster's problems for fear they won't understand. And it is true that some teachers will casually discuss a child's difficulties in front of the class, embarrassing him to the point of tears. But barring an insensitive teacher, many months of bewilderment and frustration for both teacher and child can be avoided by an early meeting and an honest sharing of information.

The meeting with the Browns helped Teddy's teacher know what to expect. She realized that Teddy's parents were willing to help her with him, and she didn't feel so isolated in the struggle to teach him.

Learning more about a child can be a joint venture for parents and teachers. As they learn from each other, they are better able to formulate realistic educational plans to meet the specific needs of the child. In fact, the federal government now mandates that every child with an identified learning disability *must* have an individual educational program (known as an IEP) developed by his parents and special teachers together.

An IEP sets out, in some detail, the child's level of functioning, his weaknesses, and the goals that are to be met in the school by the end of the year. These include behavioral, cognitive, and affective (or emotional) goals and are subject to ongoing reevaluation and revision every year. The IEPs serve as a continuing diagnosis and teaching prescription for a child. Short-term IEPs are also required in some areas, such as New York City. These need not be shared with the parents but are valuable for teachers in that they have to take a second look at whether or not their long-range goals are realistic and likely to be achieved.

It is important to note that IEPs are written in specific behavioral terms rather than in the broad generalities so frequently associated with education. A first grader's IEP might include such objectives as "John will recognize all capital letters of the alphabet and identify initial consonant sounds." (An IEP that might have been appropriate for Teddy is included [see pages 170–171] as a sample, though the forms for IEPs vary greatly from school to school.)

Throughout the fall, Teddy seemed to be doing better, and his parents breathed a sigh of relief over their decision to keep him in the regular school. Teddy's teacher even thought he might catch up with the class by the end of the year if he continued at his present pace. But he didn't. Maybe it was the bout with the flu, the long Christmas vacation, or his learning problems. In any case, everyone got jittery again in February when Teddy's achievement test results were in the lowest percentile. Then his teacher came up with the idea that perhaps Teddy should repeat the second grade with her next year. But, Teddy's parents argued,

Teddy was a good athlete and popular with his classmates at last, and it didn't seem fair to separate him from his friends. By April, Teddy had started to move forward again. His reading improved and he seemed more interested in schoolwork. In June, he was promoted to third grade.

As usual, Teddy loved the summer in day camp. He may have shied away from the challenge of a song fest or camp play, but otherwise he was a great camper. He swam and played baseball, and his self-confidence grew. Reports from his counselors were glowing and Teddy seemed relaxed and happy. His parents hated to see camp end almost as much as Teddy did.

In September, Teddy's third-grade teacher called the Browns before they could call her, suggesting a meeting with the principal, the psychologist, and her. This time it was the teacher who wondered what Teddy was doing in third grade. His second-grade teacher had spoken to her about Teddy, but she had no idea that he would be so low-functioning. "He must have forgotten a lot over the summer," she said (a problem typical of youngsters with learning difficulties). Now he was so far below the rest of the class that there was no group for him, and he seemed miserable and alone in class. He was particularly unhappy about having to work in a first-grade math book. He kept "losing" the book and telling everyone who would listen that he was sure he could join the class in their third-grade text. Everyone at the conference agreed that Teddy needed a cohesive, integrated program to help remediate his learning difference.

For the time being, Teddy was assigned to an itinerant learning disabilities specialist who would work with him one hour a day on an individual basis. Many school systems employ teachers who travel from school to school, in lieu of, or in addition to, the resource teacher. For Teddy, the itinerant teacher became an additional source of help, since he continued to go to the resource room as well.

Teddy was lucky to have so many people attending to his educational needs, and his school was fortunate in having such a wealth of resources available. Most schools in the United States, particularly in urban areas, have few, if any, ancillary services—

and many children in need of them. Youngsters with learning differences may flounder about in school for years, without benefit of diagnosis or remedial help. Then parents and teachers wonder why they act out their frustrations by misbehaving and eventually dropping out of school. While it is true that supplementary educational services are expensive, so is caring for the educational misfits of society.

Once again Teddy's parents began to look for an appropriate special class for the following year. But in March, Teddy's teacher said she couldn't believe what she was seeing. Teddy was no longer at the very bottom of the class, his attention span had improved, and she felt he could stay where he was—with help. On again, off again. Is it any wonder parents are confused? They want to do the most they can for their child, but what is that? How will he be next year or even next month? Who knows?

While Teddy's teacher enjoyed him and felt he could probably manage at least one more year in a regular class, his parents and the teacher in the resource room didn't agree. They recognized the vast difference in academic performance between Teddy and his classmates and felt that he would suffer in the competitive atmosphere of fourth grade. Although Teddy was making good progress, he wasn't learning fast enough to close the gap. In fact, in some subject areas, the gap seemed to be growing wider. Surprisingly, he was learning his multiplication tables along with the class, but he still couldn't subtract easily and was totally confounded by word problems. His difficulties with abstract thinking were becoming more apparent, and many of the concepts of social studies escaped him. Once again his immaturities were showing, and he seemed young in relation to his class.

In Teddy's community, two of the three elementary schools had learning-disability classes. Children were bused from their homes to the school at no extra charge to the family. (Most states in the United States today provide free transportation when youngsters are identified as needing special education.) With the help of the person in charge of pupil personnel services in the district, Teddy's parents visited the two special classes in the area that might have been right for Teddy. Typically, these classes are self-contained (the children stay in one classroom with their teacher for most of the day), with no more than ten to twelve children in a class. There is one master teacher trained in special education and sometimes a paraprofessional or volunteer in the class.

This kind of special class developed after World War II, primarily for mentally retarded and emotionally disturbed youngsters. Children were diagnosed, labeled, and placed in the appropriate class. In recent years, there has been much controversy among psychologists and educators over the use of segregated special classes, particularly for mildly handicapped youngsters. Several studies have shown that most children kept in regular classes do better academically and socially than do children with similar problems in special education. Since 1975, when the United States federal government mandated public education for all handicapped children "in the least restrictive environment," more children are being maintained in integrated, heterogeneous classes.

But it is also recognized that some youngsters, such as Teddy, may benefit from a more comprehensive program than can be provided in a regular class, even with the services of an itinerant teacher and/or a teacher in a resource room. When children seem to be suffering emotionally and sinking academically, their educational needs may best be met in a class with the full-time services of a teacher trained in special education.

Schools sometimes suggest special classes for more than just academic reasons alone. More frequently, children's behavior and their response to their learning problems cause them to be excluded from regular classrooms. At the point where special education was considered for Teddy, he was beginning to become clownish and even a little disruptive in school. While his misbehaving was not serious, his parents felt he needed to get away from the pressures of his class and to be with other children who were also in need of prescriptive education.

A special class can provide children with an atmosphere conducive to learning as well as a firm foundation in those basic skills that are essential building blocks to further learning. Knowing each child and his educational needs, a teacher can design a specialized curriculum. While children may remain in a special class for as long a time as needed, the goal is to move them back into the mainstream of education as soon as possible.

In thinking about sending Teddy to another school, the Browns had the expected qualms. Would he feel different, uprooted? How would his friends in the neighborhood react when they found out? Mr. Brown admitted that he even wondered whether Teddy would act different if he attended a special class with other handicapped youngsters, some of whom had severe behavior problems. Was this the right move for Teddy?

Nor did Teddy want to go to another school. Even though the going had been rough, he didn't want to leave his friends and the school he knew. (It is never easy to leave what is familiar, to change to an unknown.) His feelings made the planning and handling of his school placement even more stressful for everyone, but in the end, Mr. and Mrs. Brown felt that their decision to transfer Teddy to a special class was right.

The wisdom of a child's attending a special class can long be debated, with few reliable guidelines to follow. Each child must be looked at individually. Then it is for school administrators, parents, teachers, and learning-disability specialists to determine jointly which program or combination of programs might be the best. And even then the most appropriate plan might be optimal only for a short time.

The Browns were fortunate in finding a suitable class for Teddy in a nearby school. Many communities have no special classes at all; a school may have no class appropriate for a particular child. Then parents may have to consider sending their child to one of the many private schools, day school or residential, designed specifically for youngsters with learning problems. While these schools usually do a fine job, they are very expensive. However, according to recent federal legislation, each school district is responsible for providing an "appropriate" education for every child. If appropriate public school classes are not available for a youngster, the school district may be obliged to foot the bill for private school.

In practice, however, schools will try hard to claim that their classes or resources are adequate. Like most individuals, they are not eager to incur the burden of another large bill—unless they have to! In some instances, a parent may have to become the child's advocate and insist on the most suitable program for his child. The procedures for achieving these goals will be described at the end of this chapter.

The class that Teddy's parents and the school thought best for him was one in a public school close by. There were eleven children in the class, ranging in age from seven to nine and a half years of age. Children in classes for learning disabilities are usually grouped according to their achievement level and educational needs rather than according to chronological age or grade in school. These classes are ungraded—that is, there is no class called second or fourth grade. And it is not uncommon to find one youngster working in a fifth-grade math book, a second-grade reader, and a first-grade spelling book.

In the next few years, Teddy's parents sometimes felt as if they were going to school all over again—with Teddy. They spoke to his teachers at the beginning of each year, and they had frequent conferences at school throughout the year. The Browns were also called to school from time to time to share in the planning and decision-making for Teddy. Yes, they were very much involved with Teddy's education—and they had to be. In the process, they became quite knowledgeable in the area of learning differences, and thereby more understanding of Teddy's difficulties.

For Teddy, the next two years gave him the chance to have intensive, individualized instruction. He could learn at his own pace and his teacher worked hard to teach him the three Rs. His reading improved through a "word family" approach in which words that rhyme and are spelled similarly, such as "cat," "hat," and "sat," are taught together. This technique was most suitable for Teddy because of his limited memory for sight words. At the age of ten, he finally seemed to "break the code" of the English language and became a relatively fluent reader, who for the first time could pick up a new book without feeling frightened. He was even beginning to read a little for pleasure, but only when he found a "super-good book," as he put it. He also learned to write a paragraph, using some semblance of correct spelling and capitalization. Math was still very difficult, though, and Teddy struggled long and hard to master the process of subtraction.

The happiest outcome, however, was that Teddy seemed relaxed at school and he came home in a better frame of mind than he used to. During all of this time, although Teddy was obviously benefitting from the program, his primary goal (and perhaps greatest source of motivation) was to return to a regular classroom setting. That was his greatest wish.

After two years, the Browns and the team of specialists who had known Teddy so well made a joint decision to move him back into a regular class. Had he continued in his original school, Teddy would have been a seventh grader by now, but upon his return, he entered the sixth grade, the beginning of the middle school in his community. In effect, he had repeated a grade or lost one year. This is not unusual when youngsters return to a public school from special education. In Teddy's town, the middle school—or junior high—was in a different location from the elementary, so Teddy was off to a new start, although many of his old pals were there ahead of him.

It is difficult to tell what Teddy would have experienced had he never left his old school. Several youngsters with problems similar to Teddy's had stayed, some quite happily, others in agony. Ideally a regular class should be preferable, but realistically this is not always so. In retrospect, the Browns were not sorry they had made the choice they did, but it was impossible to measure or quantify the results. They were glad, though, that Teddy was returning to a more natural school environment.

For reentry to be successful, children need to be academically and socially prepared for the change. In the middle of his second year in special education, Teddy had begun to spend part of each day in regular classes in the school. At first these were nonacademic classes, such as music and gym, but later he joined a social studies class as well.

Then, once he moved, the middle school cooperated with

Teddy's family as much as they could, providing some of the special services Teddy continued to need. The resource room, called the study skills center, while smaller than the resource room in the elementary school, was available to him on an as-needed basis. There, the teacher, burdened with too many students to see, provided some help with difficult assignments, but she couldn't spend much time with Teddy. However, Teddy was able to take advantage of the tape library, which meant that he could *listen* to the books his classmates were reading. (Parent volunteers had taped some of the more difficult books that were required reading, such as *The Red Badge of Courage.*) And in some classes, teachers permitted him to take tests orally if he couldn't write the answers quickly or legibly enough.

Nevertheless, the departmentalized system required that Teddy work harder than he ever had before, and he often felt overwhelmed. No longer was he nurtured by a special-education teacher from nine o'clock to three. He was now forced to respond to teachers who were specialists in their own subject, but who were not necessarily knowledgeable in planning for youngsters with learning differences. Here again Mr. and Mrs. Brown had to bring their expertise and understanding of Teddy to the school.

The Browns tried to interpret Teddy's difficulties for his teachers, with varying degrees of success. Math still presented the greatest problem for Teddy, and his teacher was not very flexible. Halfway through the school year, Teddy had still not managed to pass one quiz or chapter test, although his daily homework was usually correct and up-to-date. Perhaps each test covered too much for Teddy to remember, and his anxiety probably got in the way. Finally, in despair, his parents came to the school and asked if he could possibly be allowed to study from the test itself, to have extra help from the teacher, or even to use his calculator to avoid computational errors.

Teddy's teacher wanted to help Teddy, but she was concerned that it would be unfair to the other students in the class. While this is understandable, more teachers today seem willing to make concessions for youngsters with special needs. This is surely in the spirit of individualizing instruction, a point of view on which most teachers now agree. Perhaps teachers are discovering, as many parents have, that *fair* doesn't necessarily mean *equal*. After all, the goal of giving tests should be to see how much children have learned, not how badly they have failed.

By midyear, Mr. and Mrs. Brown found that Teddy was feeling burdened by his assignments and was leaning heavily on them to get them done. His organizational and study skills were still weak, and homework was a time of anguish and frustration. The school was just not able to provide enough reinforcement for Teddy. The Browns finally decided that the boy down the street, a quiet, well-organized high school senior, might set a good example and be of some assistance with homework. Teddy, though doubtful, agreed it was worth a try.

The extra help for Teddy worked well for a while until his "tutor" had to quit his job when he got too busy with preparations for college and varsity baseball. For Teddy and his parents, this was another jolt, just when things seemed to be going smoothly again. It seems that parents of youngsters with learning problems must always be ready to apply the bandaids to each new wound, but it hurts all over again when the bandaids are abruptly removed. It's not easy to go from crisis to crisis, but somehow the learning-disabled child and his parents usually manage to get through the difficult school years.

In eighth grade, the decision was made that Teddy would not begin a foreign language, even though it was part of the usual curriculum. Youngsters with learning differences often find foreign languages extremely difficult, and it may be a good idea for them to avoid them as long as possible, or even forever. Many colleges no longer hold to the foreign language requirement for admission, particularly if they know a youngster has had learning difficulties. And if a student does elect to take a language, Spanish or Latin are usually preferred. They are more regular in syntax than French or Russian, and the spelling is more predictable.

Interestingly, Teddy begged to take a language in ninth grade. As important as it is to relieve youngsters of the burden of a language they are likely to fail, it is advisable to let them try if they want to. Motivation can go a long way toward success, and besides, there is always the fallibility of prediction. Youngsters have been known to achieve amazing heights, despite all the evidence suggesting failure. One young man who was getting poor grades in French refused to drop the subject "because I like it, even though I'm not doing well." If that is satisfaction enough for him, so be it. This boy was supported by his teacher and his parents until he finally learned enough to pass the second-year examination. Then he was content. Individual drives and determination must be admired and respected.

Teddy entered the ninth grade in his local high school a few months ago with more than his usual number of fears. He always had butterflies on the first day of school, but this year was the worst. The school seemed huge, teachers' reputations had preceded them, and Teddy was sure he wouldn't be able to handle the work. Never had he felt so small and alone! On the first day of school, he came home famished. He confessed to his mother that he hadn't had any lunch because he couldn't find his way back to his locker. His lunch was safely inside it—somewhere in the school.

Teddy is now halfway through the ninth grade. He is struggling in Spanish but he knows he has the option to drop it—with the school's blessing—if it gets to be too much for him. He is also taking a modified algebra course that will take two years to complete, rather than the usual one. Math continues to be his major stumbling block, and he is being tutored once a week after school. The state requires that he pass algebra to qualify for a high school diploma. Otherwise he would have eliminated math from his program long ago.

Teddy's English course this year is a modified one, too, emphasizing the "survival" skills he will need to know after high school. The rest of his courses are in the regular track. Unexpectedly, Teddy is doing fairly well in social studies, with an understanding teacher and the help of his tape recorder. He tapes most of his classes so that he won't have to struggle to read his own notes again later. Even his "papers" are presented orally or on tape. Teddy is also learning to type, which should be useful later on when his efficiency increases. Now he can get from one end of the building to another almost on schedule. Occasionally teachers have to remind him to stop talking and come into class, but he's usually pretty cooperative.

How far Teddy will go in a straight academic curriculum remains to be seen. His guidance counselor and his parents are searching for an area of strength that could be pursued during the rest of his school years. At this point, he is still in need of a direction to follow. Recently, his parents and I recalled that he had always shown a keen interest in his mother's vegetable garden and house plants. Perhaps horticulture and landscape gardening might provide an interesting future career for him to consider.

In addition to the academic track, some alternative programs are offered in Teddy's town that might serve him well. One option would be for him to attend his high school in the morning and a vocational center in the afternoon. There he could begin to learn the skills needed for an occupation or trade.

Another possibility is a distributive education, a rather new concept in secondary education. Students work part-time in cooperating stores and businesses in the community, earning money and high school credits for their work. For many young people, these alternative high school programs may provide not only the first taste of a successful future but also a more relevant education than the college-oriented curriculum with which so many youngsters struggle. In this country today, there is a trend toward more vocational education, and many more young people are taking advantage of this opportunity. And for students with learning differences, these alternative programs may be the best—or only—way for them to complete high school.

In retrospect, Teddy has been very fortunate in his education thus far. He received a more than adequate public education even before it was mandated by law. Until this year, literally millions of children with handicapping conditions have either received inadequate education or were excluded entirely from the public school system, solely on the basis of their handicaps. But as of the opening day of school in September 1978, this was no longer possible.

On November 29, 1975, the Education for All Handicapped

Children Act (Public Law 94-142) was signed into law by the U.S. federal government. It soon became known as the Bill of Rights for youngsters with learning disabilities and other handicapping conditions. The bill specified that as of September 1978 all handicapped children age three to eighteen must receive a free and appropriate public education. (In some states preschoolers are exempt.) The law further mandated that by September 1, 1980, the age limit would be extended to twenty-one.

The federal law also requires that states provide special education and related services to children with special needs, and it provides for financial assistance to states and local school districts to develop appropriate programs and services. Whenever possible, handicapped youngsters are to be educated in the mainstream, with nonhandicapped children. Special schools and classes are permitted only when the school district can show that a regular educational environment does not adequately meet a child's needs. Parents may challenge the decisions of state and local officials about how a child has been evaluated or placed, and the law establishes a set of procedures to be followed in such instances.

Parents should know of the following safeguards provided by law to protect the rights of their children. Under the new regulations in P.L. 94-142, parents have the right to

1. prior notice before a child is evaluated or placed in a special program.
2. read relevant school records.
3. obtain a private or independent evaluation of a child's special needs if they so desire.
4. an impartial due process hearing to challenge a decision thought to be unfair or inappropriate regarding a child's educational placement.

The new law also provides for the designation of a surrogate parent to be a child's advocate if the child is a ward of the state or if parents or guardians are unavailable. And finally, the law provides for individualized educational programs in the "least restrictive environment" for each child identified as handicapped.

While P.L. 94-142 is the most sweeping piece of legislation of its kind ever enacted, it is very complex and the implications of its passage cannot be assessed as yet. At every step of the way there will be interpretations of interpretations. And there is still much work to be done. At this writing, Congress has not voted appropriations to implement the law. State and local monies still pay for the education of the children with special needs. There is still no provision for in-service training of the teachers who will be responsible for educating a wide variety of children in their classrooms.

It will be up to the citizens of each community, as well as the educators, to implement the new law. What happens inside the schoolroom will largely depend on the dedication and the efforts of the parents of the children involved. Little that has happened in education thus far to help children with learning differences would have occurred without parental pressure. In the future, parents must continue, as always, to be advocates for their own children and for children everywhere.

Chapter 6

The Homework Question

Mrs. Pratt, the mother of one of my students, phoned early one morning to tell me of the terrible scene that had occurred the night before. Jimmy, a fourth grader, had finally decided to tackle the book report that was due the next day. True, it had been assigned three weeks before, but Jimmy had just finished reading the thinnest book he could find in the library. It was nine P.M. when he asked his mother to help him with his homework. She was annoyed to hear about the report so close to the deadline, but seeing the panic in his eyes, she reluctantly agreed to help.

After five minutes of working with Jimmy, Mrs. Pratt realized how little he knew about writing a book report and, indeed, wondered if he had read the book. Jimmy was not just asking for help; he wanted her to *do* the assignment. It was at this point that she balked and refused to help at all. She told me of the anger she expressed to Jimmy. "It's your homework, not mine, and your teacher ought to know just what you can do by yourself."

Jimmy yelled and screamed that he was "stuck" and that he couldn't go to school without the report or "the teacher will *kill* me!" For the next hour, the situation went from bad to worse. Mr. Pratt got into the act, telling Jimmy to stop crying and get to work. Jimmy finally went to bed, exhausted from crying, without having written a word of the report. Guilty and upset, his mother couldn't wait to call me the next morning to ask how she and her husband could have handled the situation differently.

The first question that occurred to me was how much had Jimmy actually learned from the experience the night before. Did he learn to write a report or at least to attempt it on his own? The obvious answer to both questions was no. He had learned nothing, except perhaps to be more afraid than ever of book reports. He also may have gotten the message that asking for help at home can start an awful row. He had written nothing, but he knew he had disappointed his parents—and himself.

Knowing that Mrs. Pratt was usually very supportive and willing to help both her sons with anything they needed, I wondered aloud why this time had been so different. Perhaps the clues were at the beginning of our conversation. First, she was annoyed (justifiably so) at Jimmy's disorganization and late start on his homework. Second, his difficulty with the assignment only highlighted the extent of his problems.

A parent can easily forget that a child is having learning problems when he doesn't bring them home. In this situation, Jimmy's mother felt angry that his disabilities were showing, and she realized she might have been punishing him for his handicap. Maybe she was also blaming the teacher for not teaching Jimmy more effectively and was saying, "Let your teacher see how much you *don't* know." It occurred to me that she found it easier to help her older son, who didn't need much help, than to help Jimmy, who really couldn't do it alone.

Most parents would agree that the emotional involvement with one's own child makes it difficult to help him with homework. As one parent said, "Homework is an activity that usually involves reading, writing, and parent testing." If a youngster does well, it is relatively easy to edit a composition or quiz him for a spelling test. In fact it makes a parent feel good to know that his child is learning so well. But when learning is a struggle and material learned one minute is forgotten the next, it is frustrating for the parents as well as for the child. This frustration is heightened when a tired parent is summoned at nine at night to help a youngster with homework that he has somehow managed to put off until the last minute. A parent's natural instinct at that point may be to remain aloof to avoid a confrontation. As a result, parents may tend to work less with their children who really need the help than with the child who merely wants a little support and encouragement.

How much should parents help youngsters with work brought from school? I think the answer becomes clearer if we ask ourselves what is the purpose of homework and what are the educational goals for a child. If the idea of homework is to reinforce skills taught at school, parents may be needed at home as facilitators or adjunct teachers. Extra practice on addition facts or the week's spelling words is something most parents can do with ease in a relatively short time. But for the child with a learning difference, understanding, patience, and even teaching *may* be needed at home. Then, as the requirements of school become greater, the homework may become unrealistic for a child. Loving it or not, a parent (or surrogate) will have to share the burden of work at home if the youngster is to succeed in school.

Jimmy's teacher had probably taught the class how to organize and write a book report, but Jimmy apparently had not mastered the technique. Perhaps he had been distracted by the noise from the playground or the radiator, or maybe his teacher talked too quickly or too softly. For Jimmy, oral instructions alone were not sufficient. He needed to be shown in detail on paper what to do in order to really understand what was involved. And with his poor memory, he would require more than one lesson before he'd even know how to begin.

Jimmy really couldn't write the first report alone that evening but he might have come a step closer by being an active participant in one his mother did with him. Children with learning differences learn more from a model than from their mistakes. I have seen it work.

Josh, in sixth grade, had a social studies assignment in which he had to outline a chapter of his textbook. He seemed quite helpless, and in two sessions, I almost did it for him, encouraging him to read aloud only the "dark print" headings to use for his outline. He did little of that first outline, but he was very proud that he could hand it in on time, along with the rest of the class. The next time he had to summarize a chapter, his mother called to say that although I had shown him how to do it, Josh still couldn't organize the material. I suggested that she or her husband help him as I had, encouraging him to identify some of the key words or salient points when he could find them. By the fifth outline, which he brought to our lesson, I acted only as his secretary, writing down what he told me was important. He had finally gotten the idea of selecting main ideas and important facts, although it was still an effort for him to do the reading as well as the writing, with any approximation of correct spelling.

I offered Josh another helpful suggestion for social studies homework. There were questions to answer at the end of each chapter. By the time he struggled through the reading of the chapter, he had usually forgotten the information, or more likely, he had not understood the material in the first place. It may sound like taking a shortcut, but I recommended that he read each question and find the answer in the text *without* reading the entire chapter first.

Josh looked at me with surprise, as if I were advocating that he cheat. Then I went on to locate the appropriate paragraph for him until he could find the information himself. (It makes sense to do this, particularly when social studies chapters are long and involved.) Then after he had completed the written work, he could read the chapter or have someone read it to him. He was able to absorb and retain the information more fully without the pressure of reading and then answering the questions for homework.

Some high school students prefer to write down key words from the questions to look for in the reading. That saves going back to find the answers in the text. They might stop to answer the questions when they spot some of the words and then continue with the reading. Many books even make a perceptive student's job easier by using the same words and phrases in the questions as in the text.

For older, more advanced students, the SQ3R is a good technique for studying or preparing for a test. The acronym stands for "skim, question, read, recite, review." First, a student glances over the material to be read, getting a general idea of what the selection is about. Then he asks himself some of the questions that might be answered in the reading. Reading the passage is next, followed by testing his knowledge, either by himself, with a tape recorder, or with a surrogate teacher at hand. A review of difficult concepts is the last step in this process. Sometimes the review can be prepared by dividing a page down the middle. Key words or questions are written on the left and the corresponding answers on the right. Then the youngster can test himself by folding the paper, keeping the answers hidden from view.

Another aid for the older student is for a parent to offer his secretarial services. For many high school students with papers to write, the mechanics of writing is the hardest part. A parent's willingness to type a theme can alleviate much of the anxiety aroused by a long assignment. And it's not a sin to correct the spelling and punctuation as you go along. Making a list of spelling words written incorrectly, to be learned at a later time, might relieve both parent and youngster of guilty feelings about the editing.

The most obvious indication of difficulty in any subject is when the books don't come home at all. "I forgot to bring my book home" or "I left my homework on the bus" are two of the most common ways a child says, "I couldn't do my homework," or "I didn't want to." The youngster who denies having homework or says he "did it in school" may be avoiding the issue. "The dog ate it" or "It must have gone through the washing machine" may also sound familiar. When any or all of these become a pattern, a conference with the teacher is indicated, since the source of the problem should be investigated.

An assignment pad sent home to be checked by parents may help structure schoolwork for a child; occasionally, an extra text-book kept at home will eliminate one excuse for not doing homework. After protesting initially, one youngster said that he really liked the "blue sheet" his school used for recalcitrant homework doers. His teachers and one parent had to sign the sheet every day. That system helped him conform to expectations, and he liked the feeling. He told his mother, "Now I *know* I can't forget, even when my mind tells me to."

I recently heard about a schoolteacher who must have done something right with respect to homework. One morning an eight-year-old girl with learning problems ran to the assistant teacher in the classroom, sobbing that she had not finished her homework the night before. The sympathetic lady tried to soothe her, saying she was sure the teacher would understand. "No," the little girl tearfully went on, "Miss Stewart said if I didn't finish my homework, she wouldn't give me any more." That teacher obviously knew where her threat would be effective.

Each subject in school presents different kinds of homework problems. One youngster made it a habit not to do his math homework. He claimed that he didn't need math to be a baseball player. Nonetheless, he and the teacher argued about his attitude with respect to his homework for the better part of a year. He usually did his social studies and English assignments, but rarely did his math. One day, I suggested that he bring his math book to our next lesson. As soon as I saw what he went through trying to copy rows of addition and subtraction problems, I knew where he needed help—not with the answers, but with copying the problems. For children with perceptual difficulties, transcribing from a math book onto paper can be a dizzying experience. This boy's columns were askew, he mixed up his signs, and then he sometimes copied the wrong problems onto the page. As soon as I wrote the problems for him, he could quickly compute the answers, with few mistakes. For that child, either a workbook-text in which he could write or a willing transcriber at home would have helped.

For many youngsters with learning differences, math is hard enough in school, but math homework can be their nemesis. First, they must be able to read and understand the directions. For some children, this is impossible. They strike out on two counts. Their impulsiveness and/or their inability to read the words makes them leap before they look. Reading problems *do* affect a child's math. Many a child has been known to do an entire page the wrong way because he couldn't or wouldn't read instructions. And if he can't decipher the word "multiplication," no knowledge of the times tables will help.

It may save anger, tears, and the need to redo an entire assignment if a parent or baby sitter reads the directions with a child and perhaps starts him on the first problem. Then he may be able to proceed on his own. I sometimes go ahead with a child in his math or spelling book, reading directions for the *next* week's work, making certain that he knows what to do on each page. It assures both of us that he will feel confident in approaching his work for the next few days.

Most parents used to feel fairly secure in their ability to help a child with second-grade arithmetic, but these days the language of the new math can confuse even the sharpest accountant. Whoever heard of "regrouping" (the new term for borrowing in subtraction), "base five," "expanded numeration," or the "commutative property"? (Yes, numerals, like executives, do commute.) Even when parents are confused by the terms, all is not lost. It's really the same old number system with new names. A brief conference with a youngster's teacher may help clear things up. And there are even some evening courses for parents on learning math the modern way.

Spelling is probably the least threatening subject for a parent-tutor. There isn't much room for parents to question how the subject is taught in school or to be confused by new methods. While children respond differently to various techniques of learning how to spell a word, I can suggest one way that seems to work for many. First, and most important, read the words to the child or have him read them if he can *without error.* If the reading of the words is hard, anticipate where he will get stuck and tell him the word first. Then have him read the list once more, telling what each word means. There is no point in a child's memorizing a series of letters without knowing what they mean. Besides, they'll be forgotten more easily if there is no comprehension.

One boy in eighth grade was trying to learn to spell the word "chaotic." He spelled it a few times, omitting or adding at least two letters each time. Finally I asked him what the word meant. He said, "Honestly, I've never heard of the word 'chā-ō'-tik.' " As soon as I pronounced it correctly for him, he knew what it meant and learned to spell the word easily.

After the words on the list are read and defined, a child should point to each letter, saying the word as he traces it with his finger. Then if he thinks he knows it, can he visualize it with his eyes closed, writing it in the air? It helps if he says the word again as he "writes" it with his finger. If he can see it on his mind's TV, he should try to write it on paper, checking afterwards to see that he is right. One more time should do it. Then do the same for the next word on the list. But *don't* try to learn more than five new words a day. Too much pushing to do "just a little more" can discourage a child, making him apprehensive about the next session.

Each day, review the ones learned before, so that by Friday all the words have been learned and reviewed for the weekly test. Sometimes children will say, "But I learn them by saying them out loud; I don't have to write them," as they repeat letter after letter orally. While this does work for some, it usually is more effective to write the words and "see" them on paper. I tell youngsters to look at a word's "face." Does it look familiar and right? Incidentally, reviewing spelling or any subject just before bedtime is supposed to make it sink in while a person is sleeping. Maybe it's an old wives' tale, but perhaps we do learn subliminally, after all.

Nothing stifles creativity like the pressure of an assignment "to be creative." Children will tell me the most original stories, fantastic or factual, but they freeze the minute they have to put their thoughts onto paper. Sometimes an exchange of ideas with someone *before* attempting to write is helpful; and pastel-colored paper, rather than stark white, can be inviting to the reluctant writer.

A friend of mine told me about her son, who could never do his English homework because he couldn't think of an idea he thought adequate. He'd sit for hours, tossing crumpled paper after crumpled paper into the wastebasket. His creativity seemed to vanish under pressure. Finally his mother, sensing the extent of his torture, made a deal with him. She said she would suggest some ideas and even supply the first sentence if he would then take over. Somehow this seemed to allay his anxiety, and he could then proceed on his own.

One girl's favorite subject was science, where she "didn't have to be imaginative." When I asked her one day what her class was studying in science, she replied, "Oh, we're not studying science, we're *doing* it!" Indeed, in many school systems, the science curriculum has been revised, making it a living experience for young students. Nevertheless, writing up an experiment and drawing a paramecium that can be distinguished from an unintentional smudge on the page may be a real challenge for a youngster whose small motor coordination is not up to par.

It is when the science teacher takes off points for neatness and spelling, though, that many an enthusiastic student gives up. That's when a parent might intervene. One teacher added insult to injury by telling his class of fifth graders that they were responsible for the spelling of all the words in dark print in the chapter. Joe, one of my students, couldn't find most of the words (he didn't know how to skim), much less learn to spell them. And if he had tried to copy them onto paper, they'd have been misspelled anyway. I suggested that the teacher give him the list of words he would have to know for the science test, which helped a little.

For some youngsters, it is the concepts of science that are difficult. They just can't envision the complex layers of the earth, for example, and they try to learn the material by rote. But memorizing is often the hardest for youngsters with learning problems, particularly when they don't understand the material they're trying to learn. Someone might have to explain it with pictures as well as with simple words for them really to grasp what happens.

It sounds as if parents are very involved with their children's homework, and indeed, parents frequently complain that their learning-disabled children are too dependent on them. One child used to say, "Come on, Mom, let's do *our* homework." Her mother finally rebelled, telling her daughter that it wasn't *her* homework—she had already passed third grade. Susie's mother was right, but where does a parent draw the line? We know that many children need help if the work required is beyond them. If the work seems reasonable, a hands-off policy can foster independence.

Too often, though, as the demands of school increase, the responsibility for initiating and doing homework shifts from the child to his parents. The youngster may hope to avoid the responsibility altogether after a while. One mother challenged her son, saying that he really wanted her to do his work for him. This nine-year-old's response was an indignant "Of course not. I have too much pride for that, but who invented homework anyway? He certainly didn't like children."

Once the responsibility for homework shifts to parents, they become involved in a power struggle with the child. And if family expectations are too high, the child cannot afford to make mistakes. It may become easier for him to stop trying than to try to please his parents. Then only his parents' nagging will bring him to the homework table, and the work never does get done in a way that is gratifying for him or his parents.

Johnny, a fifth grader, had a long history of learning problems and impulsiveness. Finally his parents, tired of their son's reliance on them for daily work, tried to establish a new policy at home. Johnny was to do all his work alone and then show it to them. Only then could he watch his favorite TV show.

On the first night of the new regime, Johnny went upstairs and dashed off his homework in five minutes flat. He hadn't read the instructions, though, and not understanding the work, wrote anything on the blank lines, just to get it over with. He was devastated when his parents insisted that he do the assignment over again, this time correctly. It took many weeks before Johnny could muster the self-control to approach his homework with equanimity. His parents learned, too, through watching him try to succeed, to be somewhat less severe in their judgment and more appreciative of the effort he was making.

The goal of independence should remain uppermost, for children's homework as well as for daily living. How much they can do on their own is a difficult but necessary question to ask oneself periodically. Many parents, as well as many teachers, are concerned that children will rely on a homework helper as a crutch once the pattern is set. On the contrary, I usually find that when a sprained ankle feels better, crutches are quickly discarded. If a parent doesn't hold onto a child too tightly because of his own anxiety, his boy or girl will let go as soon as he is able to walk on his own.

Not surprisingly, children who sense their inadequacy all day long in school feel insecure when faced with what they perceive as a task that is beyond them. The homework assigned may be appropriate and well within their grasp, but their anxiety alone makes the work seem insurmountable. Frequently, it is not the direct help provided at home but the comfort of a parent's physical presence nearby that saves the day. I have suggested to some parents that they merely sit in the same room as the child. Parents can answer an occasional question or give an encouraging "That's good work" while reading the newspaper or paying bills.

This raises the question of where homework should be done. Most parents will probably think the obvious answer is in a child's room, at his own desk, with as little noise or distraction as possible. Not necessarily. The correct answer is wherever a child feels he can work best. That may mean on the kitchen table, on the living-room floor, or in the middle of family activities. Some children really dislike being alone in a quiet room, particularly when they're doing a job they don't like—and schoolwork usually fits that description. Other children need to be separated from sibling scenes and other distractions. They should find a private corner of their own.

The father of a boy with learning problems, who also happens to be a school principal, told an audience that his son read to rock music, usually a favorite Beatles album. The boy's teacher had asked that he read for a half-hour a night, and the records in the album played exactly that long. His father added, "I never knew reading could be so loud!" But it seemed to work. The boy's parents assumed, probably correctly, that the noise of the records blocked out other stimuli or impinging thoughts, thereby improving the quality of his son's reading.

This story amused me, since I knew a boy who acted as if he'd been kicked in the stomach whenever he was asked to read. Unable even to catch his breath, he could scarcely get the words out. One day he asked if he could bring a favorite record to our lesson. It was amazing how much more easily he read with the music blaring (or perhaps I couldn't hear his mistakes?). For a long time we played records as we worked, and it seemed to have a relaxing effect. Good pedagogy? In this field, what works is valid.

For some children the distractions of rock-and-roll music or a busy kitchen can be disastrous. My only suggestion for parents of children who have trouble settling down to work is *not* to have a preconceived notion of where to do homework but to know your child and set the scene accordingly. You might need to discuss this with his teacher or another professional. Whatever you decided, don't be rigid or rule out any number of possibilities for a happy homework place.

When to do homework is no easier a question to answer than where. For some children, rising early in the morning to complete an assignment works well, while for others, the privilege of staying up for an extra half-hour at night is better. For most children, the hours before and after dinner are the best time. That way, there are no midnight surprises and a child can take some time out to play. One thing to keep in mind is your child's energy level. If he is too hungry to concentrate at five o'clock, perhaps some fruit juice and a cracker will tide him over.

Short periods of concentrated work are more effective for learning than one long sitting. This is particularly important for the child who has a short attention span or difficulty with concentration. I have occasionally used a kitchen timer to encourage a child to work for ten uninterrupted minutes before the bell goes off. Then he can "unfasten his seat belt," walk around, raid the refrigerator, or make a phone call before returning to work.

Every child reaches a point of saturation and of diminishing returns. There's an old saying: "The brain can only absorb as much knowledge as the seat can endure." When a child has spent an hour on difficult homework and is looking bleary-eyed, it is probably the time to stop and let his teacher know that he did as much as seemed reasonable for the day. She should understand.

Also, when the response to homework is anger directed at parents, books, teachers, God, and the bathroom door, someone had better check to see if the assignment is too difficult.

One father, a schoolteacher by day, found that he could help his son with homework quite successfully. (It doesn't always have to be mother.) He much preferred, though, to work with his fifth-grade son when he came home, before five o'clock. Understandably, he liked to relax after supper and go to bed early. This meant, though, that Evan couldn't go out to play after school. For him, working with his father became a punishment.

Evan's mother then asked his sister, Gail, to take over, but this didn't work either. Evan resented his sister's intervention and refused her help. He was right; it put Gail in a position of authority over Evan that wasn't appropriate. Even when big sisters are good students and "born teachers," it's usually not a good idea for them to help their siblings who may be less apt academically. It was finally decided that a high school student who lived nearby could teach Evan *after* dinner. That suited Evan perfectly and relieved the rest of the family of Evan's homework.

Most often, the task of helping with homework is left to Mother. The myth is that Father has worked hard all day and needs to relax when he comes home. But it may be Father, absent during the day, who can more skillfully avoid a tantrum over a hard assignment. And today, with more working mothers, father may be the logical choice. Of course, if either parent has had a particularly hard day, he or she is probably not the parent of choice to help with a creative story or hard-to-teach fractions.

One word of caution about father-teachers. I have noticed that once fathers begin to teach, they sometimes become over-zealous. One of my children used to say, "I don't like to work with Dad because he tells me more than I want to know." By and large, children only want to be taught as much information as they need for school the next morning. Rarely is a youngster so eager to learn that he is receptive to more knowledge than is required for class. It is usually wiser not to attempt to provide a whole encyclopedia of knowledge at one sitting. If handled well, the child will come back for more information as he needs it.

A homework helper doesn't always have to be a parent at all. In fact, it is frequently reported in psychological literature that a parent is not, and should not be, his child's teacher or tutor. A child has many teachers, but only one set of parents. One respected authority in the field, Dr. Milton Brutten, has written:

> There is rarely a parent, even one who is a good teacher of academic subjects for other children, who can be effective tutoring his or her own youngster. Parents are too emotionally involved with their children to be objective. When the mother-child relationship, or the father-child, is converted to that of teacher-child, the child in effect no longer has a mother, or a father, but only one more mediocre teacher.[1]

For many families the quote seems apt. As one mother said wistfully, "I wish there were no such thing as homework. It makes me feel stupid when I don't know how to teach Janie today's math, and then I get angry at my own stupidity. Besides, I'm sending her to school to be taught by teachers who were *trained* to teach. Then all she does is bring it back to me. It's not fair."

Another parent described the sparks that flew every time he sat down to work with his son. "I don't want it to happen, but I simply can't be patient with him. We always end up angry and screaming at each other." These are surely times when home-teaching is contraindicated.

I once believed that parents should *never* work with their own children. It was only as I greeted parents in the waiting room of my office that I began to view the matter differently. I would find myself saying to a mother or a father, "Harold and I have been working on learning to tell time. Perhaps you could continue it at home by having him count by fives and read the minutes on the clock." As long as my instructions were specific, most parents seemed very interested and eager to help. I noticed that their involvement with their children's lessons seemed to help them view their children's learning problems more realistically, without the mystery that was previously there. They were also able to see the improvement as it came. In effect, they became partners with their children in the learning experience.

In February of one year, Eric (a second grader) was referred to me by a neurologist. In light of Eric's learning problems, the doctor had recommended a special school for him, but Eric couldn't be admitted until the following September. I wanted to help Eric, but I only had one hour a week—a lunchtime at that —hardly sufficient to support Eric in his class, even for the balance of the year.

Eric's mother and I devised a plan. I would include her in our weekly sessions, after which she could follow through at home with Eric on a daily basis (with a time limit of twenty minutes). We embarked on a program that was rewarding for all of us. Eric did so well that he never did have to attend a special school, and his mother, excited by the progress he made, went into the field of special education!

Since then, I have encouraged many parents to work with their own children at home. Occasionally I have even guided parents over the telephone without seeing the child every week. While this surely would not be appropriate for all parents or even for most children, it is one of a variety of approaches that can be taken when children need assistance.

In determining how to proceed, parents must respect their own feelings and their ability (or the lack of it) to work with youngsters at home, and be guided accordingly. A parent should be a parent first, and then a teacher only if the role is mutually satisfying and not painful for parent or child.

You should expect that children with learning differences will require more assistance, more guidance, more comforting, and more help with homework than their siblings or classmates for whom learning is easier. If our goal, after all, is to help youngsters compensate for their learning problems and become successful in life, they must gain as much as they possibly can from the educational system. If this requires the extra reinforcement called homework, let's try to keep it from becoming the most dreaded activity of the day.

Chapter 7

Community Resources

As his parents, you are your child's greatest resource and most important advocate. You know him best and will provide him with the basic foundation for his future. And you are the people who will seek, and eventually find, the professionals who will help him with his learning problems. The goals are clear, but the search for the right kind of help is a continual challenge, often creating confusion for parents. It is not surprising that they sometimes imagine they are on a merry-go-round—moving, to be sure, but never reaching the objective of finding appropriate sources of help.

I once heard a speaker humorously liken the process of this search to a variation of the game of Monopoly. The goal of the game was to pass Go, having found suitable help for a youngster with learning problems with as few wasted motions and repetition of steps as possible. While most players could avoid landing on the trouble spots of Chance and Go to Jail, they frequently landed on squares marked "pediatrician," "school nurse," "psychologist," "social worker," "ophthamologist," "optometrist," "pediatric neurologist," "allergist," "educational therapist," "remedial reading teacher," "speech therapist." Though there was no card that told you to "take a ride on the B&O," there was certainly a card reading: "Take a ride on the *Reading*." Perhaps the speaker was stretching an analogy, but to a parent new to the "game" of finding help for his child, all of the professionals' offices through which his child might pass to come out an intact person, succeeding in spite of his disabilities, must seem like an endless maze.

It may reassure you to realize that even if the child in your family whom you suspect may have a learning difficulty is not yet in school, you need only consider three general areas of services. They are

1. diagnostic services.
2. educational planning and treatment for the child.
3. help for parents.

Diagnosis of a youngster's learning difference is clearly the essential first step. At the very least, an initial evaluation is required, followed by periodic reassessment. When and how should this process start? Parents should seek professional advice as soon as they have questions or concerns about a child's development or his ability to learn. Early consultation can relieve a parent's anxiety, and if treatment is indicated, the earlier it is started, the better!

The pediatrician or family physician may be the first person to be made aware of a child's problem outside of school. Until recently, children's learning was considered to be solely an educational problem, the domain of the school, and beyond the interest and concern of the physician. Parents might have been put off with the familiar "Don't worry, he'll outgrow it," and problems were not recognized until the child was safely in school. Then there was little communication between home, school, and physician. Most often, a school crisis had to occur before forces were mobilized to diagnose and help the child—and the pediatrician remained in the dark, ignorant of what was occurring.

Today, though, the pediatrician is appropriately becoming more involved with the special problems of childhood and is the right person to consult when a problem in learning is suspected. He should listen to your concerns, take a careful history of your child's development, and examine his patient thoroughly to eliminate the possibility of a progressive condition or a physical basis for the problem. An informal checklist of behaviors sometimes associated with learning differences or developmental lags that pediatricians often use is included on pages 125 and 126 as a guide. If you and your doctor have not discussed some of the behaviors on the list, perhaps you should go over them together. While there are no quantitative norms, a judgment can usually be made. If too many checks show up in the questionable column, further evaluation may be indicated. The child's symptoms would dictate whom to see. If your pediatrician is one who simply dismisses your concerns with a wave of his hand, you may want to provide him with well-chosen reading material on the subject —or to seek another, more supportive physician.

On the basis of his study, your physician may recommend an ophthalmic evaluation, a speech and language exploration, psychiatric or psychological consultation, a neurological examination, and/or further diagnosis by a learning-disability specialist. Most doctors can recommend either professionals in the area or a clinic where professionals in a variety of disciplines work together as a diagnostic team.

As parents, you might not flinch at a referral to an eye doctor, but the words "neurologist" or "psychiatrist" may upset you. This is understandable, particularly if these specialists are not part of your own experience. But be reassured, neither's examination is at all painful or uncomfortable. The neurologist consulted for a youngster with learning problems is usually looking for signs of minimal cerebral dysfunction and perhaps hyperkinesis, another name for hyperactivity. He might recommend medication for the child if it seems warranted. Documentation of a visit to a neurologist is also required in many states today in order for a child to qualify for special education programs.

A psychiatrist, who is a medical doctor, can also prescribe and monitor medication. In addition, he can assess the emotional status of a child and help with problems of home management. A psychiatric consultation does not necessarily mean that years of psychotherapy are in the offing. A psychiatrist who had evaluated a friend of mine and her son with learning problems came to the conclusion that they were mutually encouraging the dependency between them. He suggested that they go home and work on separating from each other. He offered specific suggestions and another consultation six months later, by which time many changes were seen, precluding the need for direct therapeutic

IDENTIFYING THE YOUNG CHILD
WITH A LEARNING DISABILITY
Physician's Checklist

REPORTED BEHAVIOR	APPROPRIATE / QUESTIONABLE	NEEDS FURTHER INVESTIGATION

I. AT HOME
Is child subject to

1. poor sleeping habits? _____   _____
   a. crying at bedtime _____
   b. restlessness at night _____
   c. nightmares _____

2. frequent, unpredictable temper tantrums? _____   _____

3. moodiness, irritability? _____   _____
   a. always _____
   b. after school _____
   c. weekends _____

4. stomach aches or headaches, related to school? _____   _____

5. dawdling in morning? _____   _____
   a. refuses to dress _____
   b. no breakfast _____
   c. late for school bus _____

6. complaints about school? _____   _____

7. restlessness. Is he "always on the move"? _____   _____
   a. at mealtimes _____
   b. trips to supermarket _____
   c. visits to friends _____

8. difficulty adjusting to new situations? _____   _____

II. AT SCHOOL
Is the child

1. enjoying school? _____   _____

2. interested in learning activities? _____   _____
   a. rejecting "table" activities _____
   b. refuses to "work" at home _____
   c. eager, then tunes out _____

3. learning to read? _____   _____

4. able to follow directions? _____   _____

5. able to concentrate? _____   _____

6. relating to peers? _____   _____
Teachers' comments

STOP HERE IF ALL SEEMS WELL

III. DEVELOPMENTAL IRREGULARITIES
Is there evidence of

1. delayed language   _____   _____   a. articulation   _____
   or speech   b. syntax   _____
   problems?   c. word finding   _____

2. poor judgment   _____   a. responsible   _____
   and lack of   b. accident-prone   _____
   common   c. in another world   _____
   sense?

3. impulsivity?   _____   _____

4. poor motor   _____   _____   a. balance, hopping   _____
   coordination?   b. skipping   _____
                                        c. catching ball   _____

5. immature small   _____   a. cutting, coloring   _____
   muscle control?   b. writing   _____
                                        c. self-help   _____

6. poor memory?   _____   _____

7. lack of established   _____   _____
   handedness?

IV. FAMILY HISTORY
Is there a history of

1. learning   _____   _____
   difficulties in
   immediate or
   extended family?

2. "retardation" in   _____   _____
   family?

3. problems with   _____   _____
   siblings?

4. ongoing problems   _____   _____
   in family?

V. ACCOMPLISHMENTS

1. What are the   _____   _____
   child's interests?

2. What can he do   _____   _____
   well?

intervention. Sometimes merely being helped to *understand* a problem goes a long way toward alleviating it.

A psychological assessment also gives parents a picture of a youngster's current emotional and intellectual functioning. A sensitive evaluation will help parents and professionals become aware of a child's strengths for learning and his relative weaknesses, as well as give them an understanding of how he views his world and the people in it.*

If the pediatrician recommends an academic evaluation, parents may turn to a private learning-disability specialist in the community or one who is part of a clinic team. There is no one label for this kind of specialist—learning-disability specialist, remedial consultant, and educational therapist all mean the same thing. While the testing that a learning specialist does will overlap somewhat with that done by a psychologist, the learning specialist places more emphasis on the educational and perceptual functioning of the child.

If your youngster is of school age, the school psychologist or learning-disability specialist may be the person to see to begin the diagnostic procedure. Not only are his services free to children in the school, but he can provide an important connecting link to the classroom teacher and to any special help provided in the school.

In the event that the school offers no special services and your pediatrician cannot suggest an appropriate resource in the area, there are several ways to locate one. The school district principal or superintendent may know of people to see, or you may write to any of the following national organizations. They have printed material with useful information on where and how to obtain diagnosis and treatment for youngsters with learning disabilities.

Closer Look
Box 1492
Washington, D.C. 20013

---

*Some of the diagnostic tools commonly used by psychologists and learning-disability specialists are given in the Appendix.

The Association for Children
with Learning Disabilities (ACLD)
4156 Library Road
Pittsburgh, Pa. 15234

The Orton Society
8415 Bellona Lane
Towson, Md. 21204

Though most professional people and clinics are concentrated near large cities, a careful search can usually locate well-trained specialists within easy traveling distance. The education department of the closest college or university might be a useful resource, too.

Before you take a child to see anyone, you should explain to him honestly what is about to happen. The professional with whom the appointment is made should be able to guide you as to when to tell the youngster and what to say. "We're going to see a lady who will help us find out just why school is so hard for you," or "I spoke to a man who helps children find ways to learn more easily," or merely "We think you're unhappy these days and we want to help you feel better" may be used, if they are honest. Preparation in advance of the visit is advised to give the child adequate time to adjust to the idea, to ask any questions he might have, and to work through his fears and anxieties.

One mother, nervous about telling her child he was coming to my office for an evaluation, waited until the morning of the appointment. Then, just before she was ready to broach the subject, this perceptive six-year-old asked, "Mommy, isn't there someone who could help me learn to read?" He had helped his mother break the news, but he must have suspected where he was going, although the impending visit had not been mentioned. As so often happens, children seem to ferret out the secret. They should be told, though, why they are being brought to a stranger's office and what they can expect to happen there.

The objective and only worthwhile purpose for a diagnostic

evaluation is a prescription for treatment. Pinpointing a problem is useless unless there is the possibility of doing something about it. A detailed description of the child's abilities, strengths for learning, and areas of difficulty should come from the diagnosis. A written report is usually sent to the physician and the school, and a written or oral report of the results is given to parents as well, along with recommendations for treatment. The report should include appropriate educational plans and suggestions for specialized help.

Does the youngster need speech therapy, psychotherapy, remedial reading, help with math, or even special gym? In many instances, the answer would be "all of the above," but most often that would be highly impractical. Priorities have to be determined and choices made. Does it seem more important for Johnny to learn to speak well and eliminate his lisp and slushy *s?* Perhaps so, if he is nine and self-conscious about it. Or should his reading improve before you worry about his growth in self-esteem? Many times one area affects the other. The determination of which course to follow may require a consultation among all those involved with Johnny. It is probably worthwhile to formulate ideal plans, which may then be modified to coincide with reality—that is, pressures of time, family finances, and the emotional readiness of the child and his family.

When should outside help be sought in addition to remediation in school? I have met many parents who are angry with the school's inability to deal with *every* aspect of their child's difficulties. In reality, the school can do only so much—by law and in terms of budget—to meet the special needs of each and every child. There may be times when outside help can supplement the assistance given at school. When family circumstances permit, it might be wise to seek outside help if

1. a child requires a one-to-one relationship in order to learn. This may not be possible in school, and for some children, a group of two is still a group, with built-in competition and distractions.

2. school is taxing for a child. He may need juice, cookies, and a "decompression chamber" in a homey office rather than a classroom.

3. a child needs more time to learn and more reinforcement of skills than the school can provide.

Every so often, I am asked what I as an educational therapist do in private practice. I usually say that most of my work is done with parents and teachers, and once in a while I might have to see the child! I realized long ago that I could not work in a vacuum with the child alone. No therapeutic intervention can be effective without support from family and teachers. Communication between parent and school or between parent, outside therapist, and the school is vital and should be ongoing. Parents must feel free to communicate with the professionals, asking questions and airing concerns.

The parents must feel comfortable with a professional working with their youngster. If there is resistance or a lack of cooperation, the treatment cannot be successful. It is far better to be honest with the person or people helping your child than to rush the child from one professional to another, hoping for an instant solution or cure. "Expert shopping" only makes a child feel more anxious than ever and usually does not alleviate the problem. He gets the idea that no one can help him—at least not to his parents' satisfaction. He must begin to feel he is a hopeless case.

When more than one professional is involved with a youngster, someone has to be captain of the team. A parent may have to be the self-appointed leader unless one of the professionals— pediatrician, educator, or school psychologist—will assume the role of coordinator. Frequent communication is crucial to the success of any program, and periodic reevaluation—approximately every year or two—should help keep everyone abreast of what is happening.

Finally, once your child's problems are diagnosed and he's being helped by professionals, you may want to turn to the resources most communities have available to parents. Frequently, when a child needs help, so do his parents. Even though the child is receiving specialized tutoring to help him learn, his parents may feel insecure in handling him at home. Perhaps they find him provocative and challenging, or maybe they merely feel inept in knowing how to make appropriate plans for his daily life outside of school. They also need to learn how to deal with the growing child.

A mother once called to tell me that although her son's academic problems were diminishing—he was then in the ninth grade—the situation at home was deteriorating. There were arguments about almost everything at dinner each night; she and her husband frequently disagreed about how to handle Derek. At my suggestion, they returned to the psychologist who had initially diagnosed Derek's problems when he was in first grade. She helped the Ryans see their own role in the family tug of war. She also helped them understand that Derek was an adolescent, learning difference or not, and was going through the usual developmental problems.

Mr. Ryan seemed particularly grateful for the counseling. He said he had originally responded to his son's problems with "distress, embarrassment, and anger." At the time the family sought counseling, Mr. Ryan thought he was losing touch with his son, and he felt terrible. He believed that the counseling had helped tremendously, and felt that he and his son now had an honest, close relationship.

The Ryans were fortunate to have learned about their son's problems early in his life, and to have procured a good diagnosis and a special class for Derek for a few years. And they also benefited from almost every special service offered in their community. After the psychoeducational evaluation, Derek saw a pediatric neurologist who prescribed medication for his hyperactivity and answered many of the Ryans' questions. Later Derek received speech therapy in school and individual tutoring in reading outside of school. Then came the family counseling. Expensive? Yes, but seeing the improvement in Derek and the cohesiveness of the family unit made it seem a worthwhile investment. And while great amounts of time and money were expended, the services rendered did not last longer than a few years. The Ryans also received a little help from the federal government in the form of tax benefits. According to an IRS ruling, if a child has been diagnosed as learning-disabled by a medical authority, the cost of the diagnosis, treatment, special education, and even books may be deducted as a medical expense (see the Appendix).

One additional community resource influenced the Ryans. That was the parent group they joined. There they received information about learning disabilities, shared their concerns with other parents in the same situation, and learned about additional community resources available to them. There were special camp programs, discussion groups for teenagers and siblings of youngsters with handicaps, and educational programs of interest. Perhaps most important, they also worked with the other parents toward improving programs in the school for Derek and other youngsters like him.

Parent groups have emerged as powerful advocates for children with learning disabilities in the United States today. They have been influential in fostering legislation for the education of children with learning differences in local communities as well as on the national level. Many of the innovative programs and services in school systems today came from parental pressure on the grass-roots level. In many states, parents have banded their local groups into state-wide organizations. New York's Association for Brain Injured Children, started in 1957, has been one of the leaders in the field, as is the California Association for Neurologically Handicapped Children. Today, many more states are joining the ranks of those where an association on behalf of children with learning disabilities exists. (These organizations are listed in the Appendix.) Parents' groups have helped to create a positive public attitude toward children with handicaps while influencing the education of all children.

In their enthusiasm to spread the gospel, parents and professionals, witnessing a successful treatment of a child's problems, may become quite insistent that their way is the only treatment of choice for other youngsters in need of help. They will bombard friends, neighbors, and colleagues with advice that thoroughly confuses the uninitiated. While it is always a good idea to get referrals from a satisfied customer, be wary when choosing a practitioner using a single technique promoted as *the* answer. These much-publicized and popular methodologies may help some children, but thus far, research is inconclusive and to my knowledge, there is not a single best program for all children.

Some of the current theories advocate return to crawling and creeping, visual training, and special diets as a means of attaining a higher level of functioning. There may be validity to some aspects of these theories, but they are not the magic solution to all children's problems. On the other hand, although research may suggest that some of these methods are futile, nothing, in my opinion, should be categorically debunked. Who knows? Perhaps faith in a treatment brings positive results. Professionals should, however, know and report the evidence accurately to parents—without selling one approach, but at the same time leaving room for further study.

Some of the most talked about treatments believed to affect learning are mentioned below. Most are used not alone, but to supplement educational techniques.

Optometric training is a relatively new branch of optometry, predicated on the acceptance of the relationship between visual abilities and school learning. Its practice is based on the assumption that visual perception is *learned* through developmental sequences of growth—physical, physiological, and psychological. Problems in learning can be attributed to a dysfunction in visual efficiency and sensory-motor integration. Optometrists who work in this area believe that visual organization can be trained and will affect a child's academic performance. They prescribe visual and visual-motor exercises for youngsters to improve the areas of weakness and inefficiency.

One of the early leaders in this field was G. N. Getman, an optometrist and author of *How to Develop Your Child's Intelligence.* This small book is basically a guide for parents and teachers of young children. It provides specific ideas for a readiness training program relying heavily on motor, sensory, and visual techniques. According to Getman, "Vision is involved in every mean-

ingful learning activity. Thus, vision training is intelligence training."[1]

The response of other professionals to optometric training,
especially developmental vision training, as a treatment for reading and learning problems is not all positive. Some psychologists,
opthalmologists, and educators have expressed serious doubts,
both as to the strength of the relationship between perceptual-
motor skills and success in school, and as to the efficacy of vision
training for youngsters with learning problems. Studies thus far
are conflicting, and the reported research is inconsistent. More
controlled studies are needed.

Perceptual-motor programs, such as those advocated by Kephart, Barsh, and Delacato, differ widely, but they are all based
on a relationship between motor development in a child and
learning disabilities. Proponents of these programs believe that
motor skills form the basis for higher cognitive processing and
affect a child's ability to learn to read and write. Kephart[2] advocates that basic skills should be taught in their natural order of
development to avoid what he calls the learning of splinter skills,
those abilities which lack a basic foundation. Such skills may not
be permanent and will not generalize to other learning.

Barsh's program, called the movegenic theory,[3] is based on
the belief that movement patterns lead to learning efficiency.
Youngsters who experience such motor difficulties as poor balance
or coordination will subsequently have cognitive deficits. In
Barsh's program, children receive training in developing such
motor skills as balance, muscular strength, spatial and body awareness, and rhythm.

Motor training programs, which purported to teach either
global or specific perceptual skills, proliferated in the 1960's.
Today, their popularity is waning as professionals question the
premise on which these programs were based. While it seems
logical that a child's perceptual immaturity or inadequate development may correlate with a lack of competence in reading,
much of the research of the 1970's seems to refute the idea that
perceptual-motor training has any effect on reading or academic
skills, and further, that perceptual processes can be hurried along

by means of special teaching, at least by the existing programs of today. This does not negate the value of perceptual programs for their own sake, however, particularly for young children. Improvement in motor coordination can help youngsters feel better about themselves and help make them more competent in the gym or on the playground.

The movement patterning and neurological training of Doman-Delacato stress the significance of neurological organization for learning. The theory states that the learning of academic subjects depends on a certain level of neurological organization. If a youngster has not achieved the prerequisite level because of delayed development or trauma, such learning cannot occur. The assumption of Dr. Delacato, director of the Institute of Language Disability in Philadelphia, Pennsylvania, is that one can help to organize the nervous system of a child by systematically reverting to the earlier patterns of childhood. For instance, if a child never crawled in a cross-pattern fashion (the opposite arm and leg are brought forward together), he would be taught to do so before proceeding to a higher level of coordination. Patterning consists of the precise manipulation of arms, legs, and head several times daily. Once an appropriate level of neurological organization has been established, remedial teaching may be instituted. Dr. Delacato is the author of *The Diagnosis and Treatment of Speech and Reading Problems*[4] and other books explaining his concept of neurological organization as a rationale for diagnosis and treatment.

There has been much criticism of this technique, primarily from physicians who have expressed doubts about the validity and the benefits of neurological retraining. Few experimental studies have provided positive data about this approach. On the basis of the results thus far, the theory should be held in question until more precise supportive data are accumulated.

Psychotherapy is an approach frequently recommended for children with learning differences when they have major social problems along with their learning difficulties, or when emotional factors seem to interfere significantly with their daily lives. Children with problems in learning may develop negative feelings about themselves, making it hard for them to do well in any area. Some youngsters withdraw or stop trying, while others become overly aggressive or antagonistic. A better self-concept is one goal of psychotherapy, usually accomplished through therapeutic "play" or talking with a person trained in this technique.

Occasionally a child's lack of achievement at school is erroneously attributed to emotional problems, and psychotherapeutic intervention is begun prior to testing for a learning difference. A tuned-in psychologist might be the best person to help the family recognize that an educational evaluation is in order. In some cases, a two-pronged treatment approach—educational and therapeutic—can help a child improve more quickly and more effectively than one form of treatment alone. This is particularly true if the child is anxious, fearful, or unable to handle his feelings appropriately.

Behavior modification approaches to the education and management of children with learning differences came out of the research and theories of B. F. Skinner. Behavior modification aims to change and modify observable behavior, rather than to identify the psychodynamic causes for a child's actions. Inappropriate or maladaptive behaviors are changed by manipulating a child's environment, with rewards for improvement and change. This approach is applied to educational and teaching situations as well as to social behaviors. For children who have not internalized or responded to the rewards of socially acceptable behavior, some kind of extrinsic reward system may be necessary until such time as good behavior becomes habitual. A teacher might give a child fifteen minutes of game time at the end of a day for completing all of his work on time. And a parent might reward his child by allowing him to stay up a half-hour later at night if he did his morning chores and left for school on time.

When applied to the treatment of discrete symptoms or problem behaviors, this approach is known as behavior therapy. It has been reported to be particularly successful for families who may be more concerned with changing behavior than understanding the underlying causes. Many of the principles, though, are effective for everyone.

In recent years, several treatment options have been suggested for the hyperactive child. The treatment of hyperactivity has received much attention, perhaps because the symptoms can be so difficult to live with—for the child, his parents, and his teachers. Many remedies have been proposed, ranging from behavioral to biochemical intervention. While the treatment methods are not limited to hyperactive youngsters, each claims to help reduce the level of motor activity as well as inappropriate behavior.

Medication is sometimes recommended for hyperactive youngsters with learning differences. Dexedrine, Ritalin, and other amphetamine-related drugs are usually prescribed, although some newer medications, such as Cylert, are now being used. While these drugs are essentially central nervous system stimulants, they seem to work in a paradoxical way when given to children with learning problems, having a calming, organizing effect. When drug therapy is effective, youngsters demonstrate diminished hyperactivity, improved powers of concentration, and increased ability to sit still for learning.

The drugs themselves do not produce learning—only time and teaching can do that—but the decrease in restlessness and the increased attention span can facilitate the learning process. Some physicians feel that the results obtained with these drugs may be diagnostically useful. If the treatment is effective, it suggests central nervous system involvement. However, no one would recommend use of medication unless a child's symptoms warrant it.

Traditionally, physicians have assumed the responsibility for the administration and monitoring of pharmacological treatment, but it is important that they be assisted in judging the effectiveness of the therapy by parents and teachers, who see a child on a daily basis. Dosages and even the choice of medication may have to be changed, and someone who knows the child well should be aware of its effects. Careful examinations by a physician at frequent intervals are also important, not only to ascertain the effect of the treatment, but to make sure that there are no unwarranted side effects.

Parents often ask whether youngsters on medication might

become dependent on drugs when they are older. Actually, the evidence points to the opposite—that is, adolescents who have been treated with medication in the prepuberty years have a significantly lower rate of drug addiction than others.

In a consideration of the long-range effects of medication, it has been reported. that some youngsters who are on medication for a long period of time may show a decrease in growth components—bone structure and body weight. However, most children do not remain on medication for that many years, and some researchers feel that these very active youngsters tend to be naturally small.

Megavitamin therapy has been used in recent years by those who believe that the child with a learning disability may be suffering from a biochemical disorder. One of the characteristic signs is hyperactivity. The treatment advocated consists of the administration of massive doses of vitamins and the maintenance of proper nutrition.

One of the strongest advocates of megavitamin therapy is Dr. Allan Cott, who originally applied the megavitamin theory to the treatment of psychosis. He found a significant decrease in hyperactivity, improved concentration, and an increased attention span in children being treated with vitamins. Cott reports that the therapy can last for years and that children who begin the treatment early and continue it over a long period of time generally make the greatest progress.

Some critics of this approach attribute the improvement seen in youngsters to a placebo effect. Other critics have also cautioned against prolonged use of vitamins as detrimental to health. Everyone agrees that more research is indicated.

The K-P (Kaiser-Permanente) diet has been championed by Dr. B. F. Feingold, former chief of the Department of Allergy at the Kaiser-Permanente Medical Center in San Francisco. He attributes what he perceives as an explosion of hyperactivity in recent years to the increase in the number of chemicals added to foods. Dr. Feingold has found that certain youngsters with learning difficulties react adversely to the chemicals in synthetic colorings and flavorings, and that this contributes to their hyperactivity. He claims that a diet free of such chemicals could diminish hyperactive behavior, aggressiveness, and implusiveness.

Dr. Feingold has designed a nutritionally balanced diet prohibiting foods with synthetic additives as well as those fruits and vegetables containing salicylates, natural chemicals thought to produce similar adverse effects. While a cause-and-effect relationship between food additives and hyperactivity has not yet been established to the satisfaction of all observers, many people feel that the observed improvement for children on the diet is too great to be disregarded.

Critics of this treatment hypothesize that any improvement noted may be the result of the additional attention paid to the child's physical well-being by his family. While this may be questioned, there is little doubt that the diet involves a good deal of extra work for the family cook. I have also heard mothers complain that for the child with social problems, this regime may isolate him even more. He can't even enjoy the goodies at a birthday party! At present, several studies of the effectiveness of the diet are being conducted, but the results are still inconclusive and skepticism abounds.

From these brief descriptions, it is clear that behavioral interventions for youngsters with learning differences include a wide variety of techniques. Because of limitations in research thus far, the question of the effectiveness of the various approaches remains largely unresolved. It may be reassuring for parents to remember that regardless of the treatment used, a learning difference is usually not progressive—that is, it doesn't become worse. And with appropriate diagnosis and intervention, the chances are good that there will be improvement. Moreover, even when parent and child are being helped and supported by a cooperative network of professionals and community resources, it is important for a parent to be aware that the natural growth and development of the child is perhaps their best ally.

Chapter 8

What about the Future?

What does the future hold for your child with a learning difference? What a difficult question! Perhaps the most predictable quality about a learning difference is its unpredictability. In the course of living with a learning-disabled child, most parents learn the hard way to expect the unexpected, the good moments as well as the disappointing. A youngster may occasionally come home with an A on a social studies test he was sure he'd fail, although more frequently the reverse is true. Very little in these children's lives can be counted on to remain stable for very long. Rarely does a family know the ease and comfort of the status quo. This is probably what creates the most anxiety for the child and his parents. It is not easy to live with uncertainty, and the families of children with learning problems seem to live with an almost continual stream of unanswerable questions, decisions, and all-too-frequent regrets and recriminations.

If a youngster is retarded or physically handicapped, his daily life is fairly predictable. His parents have an idea of what they can expect two years in the future. Educational and recreational goals can be planned accordingly. While the heartaches are surely no less acute, there is at least some assurance that plans made in good conscience will still be appropriate next week, and possibly even next year. Not so for the youngster whose major problems are in learning. A word learned one day may be forgotten the next, and a class placement that is appropriate one month may seem totally wrong a few weeks later. Even a school selected with great care may seem unsuitable before the year is over. And long-term educational and vocational goals are even less predictable.

It is natural for parents to ask a professional, "What of the future? Will he go to college? What is his potential?" And it may be just as natural for professionals to want to sound sure of their answers, to give parents something to count on. I have no statistics on the accuracy of predictions for children with learning problems, but I think it's safe to assume that forecasts for these youngsters are no more reliable than long-range predictions about the weather. Perhaps in the future, with more refined techniques, our forecasting in both areas will improve, but for now, predictions for children's futures must be made with special care and revised frequently, if they are to be made at all. Families will be guided by what they hear, and professionals have to be cautious in their prognostications for the future. The repercussions may be too great if they are wrong.

Ginny, who is nineteen now, first saw a neurologist when she was not quite seven. He confirmed the diagnosis of "central nervous system dysfunction. . . . with disabilities in both receptive and expressive language." He recommended that Ginny be taken out of public school and enrolled in a special private school where teachers would be understanding of her learning problems. He shook his head gravely as he told the little girl's parents that they must be prepared for Ginny to be dependent on them for years to come. Chances were that Ginny would never go to college; indeed, she probably would not finish high school—at least not in public school.

This renowned physician was probably right in his neurological assessment of Ginny. The only thing he forgot to take into account in his evaluation was Ginny's fierce determination, her will to succeed, and the support of her parents. From second grade on, Ginny worked hard, with the help of an excellent tutor. She read every day at home and did her homework faithfully. She learned in spite of her learning problems. Her teachers in school were impressed with her effort to succeed, and they helped her too—before school, after school, even at lunchtime. To everyone's surprise, Ginny graduated from her local high school—on the honor roll—and is now doing well as a sophomore at college. How many years of anxiety for Ginny's parents might have been avoided had the physician only said, "The future doesn't look promising now, but I really don't know. These problems tend to be difficult to predict." He might also have reassured Ginny's parents that learning problems are self-limiting. They usually don't get much worse than when they are first recognized if there is proper intervention.

Another young girl, a few years older than Ginny, took matters into her own hands when her future looked bleak. She had always had an impossible time in school, even with remedial help. She finally attended a special class where she still had to struggle to learn. Her mother died after a long illness when Judy was eleven, and Judy had little guidance or support from her father. No one seemed to expect much of her.

Judy remembers coming to the conclusion when she was about thirteen that she could "never be an English teacher," with her problems with reading and spelling, so she decided to develop her modest skills in art. Perhaps because she started years ahead of her peers, these skills burgeoned into an impressive art portfolio while she was still in high school. Ultimately she was accepted into a school of fine arts, from which she has just graduated, with the prospect of a good job as a layout artist in an advertising agency. She still can't read very well and rarely chooses to do so for pleasure, but she is independent—and proud of her accomplishments.

While the predictions for Ginny and Judy were wrong, few would complain about the outcomes. Theirs were among the pleasant surprises. However, predictions can lead to terrible disappointment as well. Professionals may build parents' hopes when a child is young, only to leave them disheartened when the expected gains are not achieved.

As an infant, Brian was very slow in his development. He wasn't walking at two and a half, and at three he still wasn't talking. The pediatrician, together with a consulting psychologist, assessed his problems and called them "developmental lags." "Brian will be fine," the doctors said. "He is just growing slowly."

Brian finally learned to walk and talk, but his pace of learning other skills never did quicken. He repeated kindergarten but was still unable to say the alphabet or write his name in first grade. When the school psychologist suggested a special class placement, Brian's parents objected, maintaining that the doctors had said Brian would catch up eventually. It seemed logical for him to stay among "normal" children while he was catching up.

Brian's parents, I think, had visions of his making a spurt, of his suddenly becoming average for his age. It was infinitely harder for them finally to accept Brian's limitations, which probably would not go away, at least not in the foreseeable future. Their hopes had been raised by the experts; besides, in all probability they had wanted to be convinced.

When I saw Brian in the ninth grade, he told me: "School is so hard. I've always hated it. Everyone in my class always thought I was dumb and I think I am too. Even if I could finish high school, I can't believe anyone would give me a job. So what's the use?" Brian and his parents were discouraged by the years of failure and the hopes that had not materialized. But what to do? Where to turn?

Perhaps it would have been helpful for Brian and his parents to realize that the school years are the hardest. Once they are over, the differences among people are more easily accepted and most adults seem to function in spite of their learning differences. They eventually find careers that minimize their disabilities and that give them a sense of accomplishment. While it is true that for youngsters such as Brian, a learning disability becomes a *living* disability, not confined just to school, those years eventually do come to an end.

In a recent clinic conference, a psychologist, pediatric neurologist, and I were telling parents the results of our evaluation of their eight-year-old son. The boy had a rather severe learning difference, with deficits that made it hard for him to learn through any particular area of strength. He would undoubtedly find school hard for some time to come.

At the end of the meeting, the parents asked us to give our opinions as to the prospects for their son's future. We all agreed that while we couldn't predict with any degree of reliability, we could easily picture this child as an independent, well-functioning adult. With his charm and average ability, he would probably handle adult responsibility well. It was only the next ten years or so that concerned us. How to preserve that personality and the will to learn?

This boy was one of seven children in his family. His mother, a vivacious lady with a good sense of humor, didn't seem to be getting gray hair from having three children with learning differences and many crises to handle. The professionals at that conference were, I think, as interested in *her* ability to manage her family with such equanimity as they were in her son's problems. I wondered aloud at her capacity to keep so cool and composed. She replied that she had developed her own philosophy. "I figure that anything my children will learn to do by the time they're twenty-one, I don't have to worry about now." That eliminated many concerns!

Having provided early intervention, appropriate remediation, and even special programs during the school years, parents may be tempted to relax when their children reach adolescence, content that they have done everything possible. However, it is also the responsibility of parents and professionals to help youngsters plan for their continuing education and choice of career. It is important to provide as many options for them as possible. Only in this way will we ensure that fewer people than in the past will fall between the cracks.

Until recently, little attention was paid to the learning-disabled adolescent or young adult. Educational planning and resources diminished sharply in relation to the evolving needs of the maturing teenager. Parents and professionals assumed optimistically that with early intervention, most youngsters would be comfortably in the mainstream—socially and academically—by the teen years, their learning problems outgrown or forgotten. With an increasing number of these children reaching adolescence and adulthood, it is becoming more apparent, though, that many of the earlier problems persist well beyond the early teens. Learning differences don't suddenly disappear; they frequently leave scars and residual problems which remain even into adulthood.

Loretta couldn't wait to finish high school. She was still having a difficult time settling down, even in tenth grade. When she was young, the doctors had said she would outgrow her hyperactivity by adolescence, but she really hadn't changed that much. At five, she raced nonstop through the supermarket; at fifteen, she had a hard time sitting through her classes. She no longer ran around the classroom, but she continually drummed her fingers on her desk or rhythmically kicked the seat in front of her. She was still impulsive, racing through homework assignments with little thought as to whether an answer was right, and she seemed as disorganized as ever. She was always losing her books and forgetting where she left her belongings. Her parents realized that these behaviors were probably the current manifestations of her former learning problems, but that didn't make living with her any easier. Her mother once said in exasperation, "By the time she's thirty, we'll probably have a mature twelve-year-old. Some days I just don't have the energy to give what it takes to help her through the day." Loretta's parents hoped she could finish high school, but they had no illusions about an academic future for her.

Loretta was fortunate in attending an urban high school that provided early opportunities for vocational experiences. She found, strangely enough, that when she was cutting and styling hair, she was calm, resourceful, and creative. For the first time, she had a sense of purpose and a goal in life. Her parents were delighted.

Some parents, though, are overly ambitious for their children, deciding on high educational goals for them. They subject their youngsters to years of intensive remedial programs in the hopes of dissipating their learning problems earlier and faster. These youngsters may have little opportunity to develop any interests of their own or even to make friends. All their energies are absorbed in their struggle to compensate for their difficulties in learning. Goals can be set too high and even achieved at too high a price.

I'm thinking of Raymond, whose parents were both in professional fields. They spared no expense to provide intellectual stimulation and specialized training for their son through the school years. Despite predictions to the contrary, Raymond did learn to read and write; he even became a successful student in high school. Everyone was delighted when he was accepted at a relatively prestigious college following his graduation.

His father knew something was wrong, though, the next fall, when his son called home several times weekly "just to talk." Raymond's anxiety seemed to be building, his stuttering increased, and he didn't sound very happy. He complained that he was working very hard, but his grades weren't showing it. He was having the most trouble with an English literature course that required reading at least one book each week.

When Raymond's parents went to visit him for parents' weekend, they found that he was miserable. In addition to the academic stress, he had not been accepted into a fraternity and had almost no social life. Raymond admitted that he felt like an outsider and confessed that, more than anything, he had hoped for a good social life at college.

One evening during the long weekend, Raymond invited his only two friends at school to join his family for dinner. The evening was a great success, and his parents were pleased. They realized almost immediately, though, that both of Raymond's friends also had obvious learning problems. Was this merely an accident or a matter of natural selection? We know how hard it is for some learning-disabled youngsters to make friends. Perhaps Raymond's self-consciousness about his learning or his poor self-image led him to seek out young people with similar problems.

Eventually Raymond's parents and I wondered just why he was going to college. Was it his desire, his wish to please his parents, or his fear of disappointing them if he didn't? What was college going to prepare him for? And was it worth it? No one had yet tried to determine what Raymond really wanted or what he was good at. A battery of vocational and interest tests might have been more worthwile for him—and less expensive—than a B.A. degree in his pocket.

Some youngsters, as well as their parents, cling to unrealistic goals. Chris was sixteen, still in ninth grade, and his academic skills were extremely low. He'd had learning difficulties all through school. He should never have taken a foreign language, but he insisted on taking French. He was also in an algebra class, although math was one of his weak points. He still wasn't sure of his multiplication tables and couldn't remember the process of long division. As might be expected, Chris was having a rough time, but he rationalized his Fs by saying he was bored in the modified classes. He told the school administrators that he was sure he could do better in more advanced classes. He also wanted to go to a four-year college, but of course was unrealistic about his chances for admission.

There is an enormous difference between working hard to accomplish miracles and merely wishing for those miracles to happen. Parents owe it to their children to support them in their efforts to achieve goals but to dispel the fantasies that are only that and nothing more. One young man who had been helped to achieve small successes began to be more realistic in his goals and in his appraisal of himself. He told his therapist, "I used to be Superman, but now I'm just Robert." Everyone enjoyed him more that way.

If a family is realistic, there are usually many options open to youngsters with learning differences. As I think about future prospects for boys and girls with difficulties, I'm struck by the fact that they have almost, if not quite, as many options as youngsters without learning disabilities. It would be unrealistic for the child who cannot read to aspire to become an English teacher, but he or she might be successful as a draftsperson or an engineer. Kathy Peterson Rice, a dyslexic, who struggled all through school because she could barely read, eventually graduated valedictorian of her class in Columbia's School of Engineering and Applied Sciences. She used ingenious ways to work around her disability and finally achieved what often must have seemed an impossible goal.

Not everyone has the ability, the motivation, or the stamina to achieve what Kathy did. But there are many alternatives for young people who have residual learning problems. As I've said, finding appropriate choices is an important part of educational planning, and parents and professionals would do well to direct some of their efforts toward earlier introduction of educational and vocational information into the school curriculum. In the last few years, many materials designed to instruct younger students about possible careers have appeared on the market. These games and kits provide the student with simulated work experience while they describe the skills and abilities necessary for success in each field.[1] While most of these materials are too expensive and elaborate for home use, they do belong in the classroom. By exploring possible opportunities for the future at a young age, learning-disabled children can gain a better awareness of the world outside of school. But parents and teachers must help with the next step: making sure that this new awareness is used to guide the children toward realistic expectations rather than commonly accepted goals.

Whether a youngster can complete high school in an academic program depends on many factors, among which are his aptitude, motivation, and the severity of his problems. School doors should be kept open as long as possible, though, even when a young person tries to close them behind him in frustration. It is usually better for him to remain in school than to attempt to enter the job market untrained and ill-prepared. Even though the law says he may leave school at sixteen, the learning-disabled youngster may need *more* time in school rather than less. The immature nineteen-year-old may still be adding to his maturity and to his core of skills as a senior in high school. His age should not be a reason for him to leave school.

Many youngsters with a history of learning problems—and even without—give up on themselves during the high school years and expect their parents and teachers to do the same. They threaten to leave school, convinced that they cannot succeed in an academic system in which they feel so alone, so incompetent, and so miserable. Their parents may also encourage them to leave school when the cut slips and the failure notices come home. "After all," they say, "what is he really accomplishing in school?" Trying as it might be, those who care must continue to be caring and supportive of the learning-disabled adolescent. They need other people to have faith in them even when they lack faith in themselves.

On the other hand, college entrance is the goal for an increasing number of young people with learning problems who have managed to survive in academic high school programs. Some want to go because their parents and friends graduated from college; others, because of the myth that no one can achieve success in the United States without a college degree. Perhaps because of the expense of higher education today or the overabundance of educated job seekers, this idea is rapidly losing favor, giving young people more freedom of choice.

When students with learning differences apply to college, they may have more than the usual number of questions and doubts. Understandably, they (and their parents) are concerned about their ability to meet the challenge of a college program in light of their academic and social difficulties. Some of the questions students frequently ask are:

Should I tell the colleges to which I am applying that I have a learning difference?

The answer depends on the degree of the disability. With greater acceptance of learning differences at both secondary and college levels, the numbers of young people attending schools of higher education will continue to grow. Now students can—and should—be honest with college admissions offices about their learning problems. After all, the college that would penalize a prospective student because of his disabilities ought not to be his first choice. According to Section 504 of the Rehabilitation Act of 1963, qualified persons with specific learning disabilities may not be denied admission or be subjected to discrimination.

How will I ever be accepted anywhere with my low SAT scores? Maybe 320 is a fine batting average, but it won't impress a college.

Knowing that learning-disabled students may not test well, many schools will balance test results with grades and teacher recommendations. Some colleges today will even accept an individually administered IQ test (usually the WISC-R) in lieu of SATs. Guidance counselors should request this if it seems warranted, since there doesn't seem to be any hard and fast rule. The assumption behind this individualized testing is that given native intelligence and the *will* to learn, the student will be able to succeed in college.

If I take the SATs, should I take them orally or untimed?

Students with identified learning disabilities are permitted to take the SATs in special ways,[2] but since the accommodation to their learning problems is recorded on their school records, guidance counselors are divided about the wisdom of this special testing. Some claim that students do not usually do significantly better, while others see the benefits of taking the tests without the pressure of time. It is my feeling that if a student cannot read well under pressure, it is worth the price of being identified as learning-disabled. He'll probably be accepted anyway if he qualifies.

Will professors at college understand my learning problems?

Again, it depends on the schools and the extent of the problem. In colleges that attract students with learning differences, accommodations are more likely to be made. In fact, some schools even make remedial courses available. However, unlike in the earlier grades when parents could be advocates for their children, college students will usually have to interpret their own problems to teachers and plan accordingly. I know a few college students who have advised professors that they work too slowly to complete an exam during one class period. Compromises are usually made, although one professor was heard to respond, "Bill, my boy, what you need is more self-confidence."

Do I read well enough to keep up with the work at college? And if I do read slowly, can I manage?

A great deal of reading *is* required in most four-year colleges, except in certain fields, but perseverance will help. Just as in elementary and high school, a college student with a disability may have to work harder than most to do well. He may also have to select his courses carefully, eliminating some of the heavier reading courses or balancing his program with easier ones.

What about writing papers? I have learned to write fairly well, but it takes me so long to proofread my own work.

At some time prior to college entrance, I think *every* student, learning-disabled or not, should learn to type. For many, it may be the only way to write papers that teachers can read. Also, less proofreading may be needed, since separating ideas from the handwriting frequently improves spelling. In addition, skill in typing might open the way to employment opportunities after graduation from school.

College entrance is usually possible today, even for high school graduates who have taken modified courses, no foreign language, and untimed SATs. Youngsters with learning differences can be found on many campuses, ranging from local community colleges to Harvard. And some schools are particularly interested in students with learning disabilities, providing specific programs and assistance for those with special learning needs. A few of these schools are listed in the Appendix, but the list is growing every year. Others may be found by writing to the Association for Children with Learning Disabilities (ACLD).

Community colleges throughout the country, with their open enrollment and variety of courses, are frequently seen as appropriate schools for the learning-disabled student who wants to continue his education after high school. Many offer vocational training programs as well as academic courses. For students not comfortable with a four-year commitment to education, a two-year college can be a viable alternative. The credits earned can usually be applied toward a bachelor's degree if the student transfers to a four-year school.

A significant number of students elect vocational or technical programs after high school rather than college. Those who lack ability in language areas, for example, may discover that they have talents for electronics, bookkeeping, or the culinary arts. To better serve these students, teachers in vocational programs must be aware of their special needs and be ready to help them develop their potential. Otherwise, they may fail here too.

While most young people with learning differences eventually do make it in society, some do not. Even as adults, they may continue to require a sheltered environment. There are halfway houses, group homes, and special facilities where individuals can live, work, and find company among others with similar needs. For a few, the need for a protected environment after high school is only temporary, until they mature. Just as many of them didn't learn to read until two or three years after others of their age, so, too, they may need more time to become adults, able to live independently.

One young man, a handsome, strapping six-footer, became depressed in the last few weeks of college. He was worried about his future after graduation. He asked me, "How will I make a living, if I can't read and write well? Who will hire me?" He said he had finally decided to apply to graduate school (he didn't even know in what field), admittedly to stay out of the job market for a while longer. While school was a terrible struggle for him, he felt too insecure to attempt to join the adult world. Actually, he might have been right in his self-assessment, although I doubt that graduate school was the answer to his problems. I, too, thought of him as much younger than his years. He seemed a typical sixteen-year-old in his thinking and in his emotional reactions. Perhaps he did need more time to grow up before assuming adult responsibilities. A volunteer job in the community with supervision or an apprenticeship might have bridged the gap for him between the protective atmosphere of school and the world at large, and would have been less of a strain financially.

So long as young people with learning differences are in school or are involved in special programs, they are relatively easy to observe. But what becomes of them when they go out into the adult world? No longer is their progress followed by teachers, guidance counselors, or researchers. Little is known about the adults in our society for whom learning was a struggle, and there are no precedents for others to follow. It is only now that the first generation of children with identified learning differences has grown up. Indeed, many parents today only become aware of their own learning disabilities when their children's problems are identified. As adults, they have been actively employed as productive members of their communities, despite their inability to spell and their dependence on pocket calculators. Lagging academic skills don't necessarily interfere with daily living, once out of school.

I have several friends who must have had learning problems as children. They still seem somewhat clumsy in their movements, forget names familiar to them, or cannot find words with which to communicate ideas. But I merely regard them as awkward or inarticulate when I pass them on the street or join them for dinner. I don't say to myself: "There's a person with a learning difference." Most of them are intelligent, responsive people who are interesting and fun to be with.

Perhaps my friends were the fortunate ones among the learning-disabled population. They may have been more able—or more determined—to succeed. And maybe their families somehow understood and supported them as children, even without much knowledge of their learning problems. But, for unaccountable reasons, we hear of adults for whom life has not been so rewarding. Perhaps their frustrations with learning caused them to become angry, disillusioned people who act out against society. At least one recent study indicates that many adults for whom there was no intervention early in life still have traits characteristic of the learning-disabled child. They exhibit moodiness, restlessness, outbursts of temper, and difficulty sustaining relationships. All the adults in that study had a poor self-concept and most expressed a pervasive feeling of unhappiness, lack of fulfillment, and discontent.

Knowing an adult suffering the effects of a learning problem can make the problem loom larger than life. When Ronald's learning problems were recognized, his mother seemed unduly anxious and upset. She finally admitted that she was afraid that he would follow in his father's footsteps. Her husband, a sensitive, caring father, had difficulty holding down a job. He and his wife felt that his learning disabilities were responsible. He had the usual residual difficulties with writing, spelling, and math, but he also found it hard to concentrate and to learn new concepts in business. He thought little of himself and was anything but cheerful.

This man's learning disabilities also affected his family relationships. He depended on his wife to manage all the family funds and to make important decisions—and even to help him keep his job. He didn't trust his judgment or his ability to plan wisely for himself or his wife and children. What we are beginning to realize, perhaps, is that just as one child's learning difference affects the entire family, so may a parent with similar problems disturb the family system.

I recently attended a meeting, I think the first of its kind, at which the problems of the learning-disabled adult were considered. Two of the speakers addressing the meeting had learning problems. One of them admitted that he became angry and even jealous of his children when they received remedial help that he had never had.

I have also read about a family in which the father was unable to read. He kept a veil of secrecy over his deficiency, and because of his fear of being discovered, was emotionally distant from his children. His frustation and feeling of hopelessness pervaded the family, and his children responded with anger and detachment.

Knowing this, all of us who are involved with the development of children should try to aid future generations of people with learning differences. Rather than placing all the emphasis on the education of the *child*, we would do well to focus on family involvement and treatment. Professionals in medical, educational, and psychological services must work together to help parents

1. find appropriate health services when their children are young.

2. locate facilities for early identification and treatment of children felt to be at risk.

3. understand their own feelings and accept those of their children.

4. be honest and forthright with their children about their problems and their behavior.

5. recognize the possible effects of a child's learning difference on the family.

Most of all, parents can help their child with learning problems by accepting the child for himself, by seeing him as a person with good traits and bad, only one of which is his learning difference. He is, after all, just a child with a difference in the way he learns. He's not a learning disability with a child attached.

It may hurt to have a learning difference, but it shouldn't hurt to be a child.

Notes

Chapter 1

1. Robert Rosenthal and Lenore Jacobson (1968) studied the effects of teachers' expectations on youngsters' achievement. They found that expectations based on a student's family background, information from teachers and school records, and difficulties in handling children's behavior negatively affected the teachers' opinion of the young learners, and in turn, their teaching.
2. Marianne Frostig, the Marianne Frostig Test of Visual Perception Press, 1964. Remedial programs were based on findings on the screening, and claimed to strengthen weaker visual-motor areas in a young child.
3. In his book *Why Your Child Is Hyperactive,* Dr. Ben F. Feingold discusses why there are many more hyperkinetic and learning disability children than in the past. He thinks many of their problems are in large part due to the consumption of food additives—artificial flavorings and colorings.
4. Louise B. Ames, *Is Your Child in the Wrong Grade?* New York: Harper & Row, 1967.

Chapter 2

1. Doreen Kronick, *Three Families.* San Rafael, Calif.: Academic Therapy Publications, 1976, p. 63.

Chapter 3

1. Elizabeth Vreeken, *One Day Everything Went Wrong.* New York: Young Readers Press, 1969.
2. Richard A. Gardner, M.D., *Psychotherapeutic Approaches to the Resistant Child.* New York: Jason Aronson, 1975, Chapter 6.
3. Mary Rodgers, *Freaky Friday.* New York: Harper & Row, 1972.

Chapter 4

1. Dr. Benjamin Spock, a pediatrician and an author of several books on child care, has been a parents' supporter and guide for more than a generation.
2. Dr. Arnold Gesell has authored books on normal child development. He was probably the first to outline the physical and behavioral stages through which most children pass at approximately the same chronological age.
3. Judy Blume, *Tales of a Fourth-Grade Nothing.* New York: Dutton, 1973, Chapter 5.

Chapter 6

1. Milton Brutten, Ph.D., Sylvia Richardson, M.D., and Charles Mangel, *Something's Wrong with My Child.* New York: Harcourt Brace Jovanovich, 1973, p. 127.

Chapter 7

1. G.N. Getman, *How to Develop Your Child's Intelligence.* A Research Publication, 1962, p. 106.
2. Dr. Newell C. Kephart, educator, psychologist, and author, is a

member of the Department of Psychology at Purdue University. He has written several books, among which are *The Slow Learner in the Classroom, Success Through Play, and Learning Disability: An Educational Adventure.* Dr. Kephart was an early advocate of perceptual-motor training.

3. Ray Barsh, Ph.D., originated the movegenic theory. For several years the director of the Easter Seal Child Development Center and the Workshops for the Jewish Vocational Service of Milwaukee, he and his staff developed an evaluation, training, and counseling program for brain-injured children and their parents.

4. Carl H. Delacato, Ed.D., *The Diagnosis and Treatment of Speech and Reading Problems.* Springfield, Ill.: Charles C Thomas, 1963.

Chapter 8

1. Several current vocational games and kits were reviewed in the *Journal of Learning Disabilities,* Vol. 10, no. 5 (May 1977), pp. 264–268.

2. For more information on College Board testing for learning-disabled students, write PSAT-NMSQT, Box 589, Princeton, New Jersey 08540

Bibliography

There have been many recent publications about learning disabilities, and more are being written every day. While no single book has all the answers to the difficult questions that arise, the literature can expand our present knowledge about learning differences and even revise current approaches to challenging problems. The following books, pamphlets, and journals are offered in the hope that they will provide some useful information to the reader.

Books

Anderson, L., ed. *Helping the Adolescent with the Hidden Handicap*. San Rafael, Calif.: Academic Therapy Publications, 1970.
Articles by professionals working with adolescents with learning problems. The book covers a wide range of subjects, touching everything that affects the life of the learning-disabled adolescent.
Baratta-Lorton, M. *Workjobs for Parents: Activity-Centered Learning in the Home*. Menlo Park, Calif.: Addison-Wesley, 1975.
Describes manipulative activities designed to help develop language and number skills for preschoolers, as well as more general skills, such as eye-hand coordination and observation.
Beadle, M. *A Child's Mind: How Children Learn during the Critical Years from Birth to Age Five*. Garden City, N.Y.: Doubleday, 1971.
Focusing on the relationship between heredity and environment, this book deals with the hows and whys of learning. Research findings are described in lay person's terms.
Bricklin, B., and P. Bricklin. *Bright Child—Poor Grades: The Psychology of Underachievement*. New York: Delacorte Press, 1967.

The authors, both psychologists, define the underachiever, discuss the causes of underachievement, and suggest steps parents can take to help their youngsters perform better in school.

Brutten, M., S. Richardson, and C. Mangel. *Something's Wrong with My Child.* New York: Harcourt Brace Jovanovich, 1973.

A practical, informative book for parents about children with learning problems. The physician's role, medication, and sources of help are discussed. A list of university-affiliated facilities is also included.

Cantwell, D.P. *The Hyperactive Child.* New York: Spectrum Publications, 1975.

This book gives a comprehensive overview of the topic of hyperactivity: causes, symptoms, and treatment options.

Chess, S., with J. Whitbread. *How to Help Your Child Get the Most Out of School.* New York: Doubleday, 1974.

The authors talk to parents about their role in their children's education and offer practical suggestions for handling some of the problems that arise. The pros and cons of day care, underachievers, fads in diagnosis, and competition are some of the issues discussed.

Clark, L. *Can't Read, Can't Write, Can't Talk Too Good Either.* New York: Walker & Company, 1973.

A mother's account of how she obtained professional help in her fight against her son's dyslexia. She tells the story of her findings and successful treatment in overcoming his disability.

Cohen, D. *The Learning Child.* New York: Vintage Books, 1973.

Not specifically for or about children with learning problems, this book provides guidelines for parents and teachers about educational objectives and realities for all children.

Crosby, R.M.N., and R.A. Liston. *The Waysiders: A New Approach to Reading and the Dyslexic Child.* New York: Delacorte Press, 1968.

An informative book about dyslexia in nontechnical language. The authors described how normal children learn to read and suggest guidelines for teaching the child with problems.

Cruikshank, W. *The Brain-Injured Child in Home, School, and Community.* Syracuse University Press, 1967.

The author presents classroom techniques to help special children learn. Although some of the material presented is technical, there is also some useful advice for parents.

DeHirsch, K., and others. *Predicting Reading Failure.* New York: Harper & Row, 1966.

A preliminary study that recognizes those children at preschool age who will encounter academic difficulties later on. A diagnostic instrument to predict reading failure is included.

Ellingson, C. *Shadow Children.* Chicago, Ill.: Topaz Books, 1967.

Written primarily for parents, this book defines learning problems and discusses methods of identifying and treating children. A directory of clinics, listed by state, is included.

Engstrom, G., ed. *The Significance of the Young Child's Motor Development.* Washington, D.C.: National Association for the Education of Young Children, 1971.

Physical education specialists and early-childhood educators explore the role of motor development as it relates to the total development of the young child.

Feingold, B. F. *Why Your Child Is Hyperactive.* New York: Random House, 1975.

The author, an allergist, describes the behavioral and learning problems caused by artificial flavorings and colors in food. Ways to help this condition and sample menues on the K-P diet are suggested.

Fraiberg, S.H. *The Magic Years: Understanding and Handling the Problems of Early Childhood.* New York: Scribner's, 1965.

A useful book about all children. The author describes personality development during the first five years of life. Some of the typical problems emerging at various stages are discussed.

Freeman, S. W. *Does Your Child Have a Learning Disability?* Springfield, Ill.: Charles C Thomas, 1974.

The question-and-answer format of this book gives it clarity. The author summarizes basic knowledge about learning disabilities, symptoms, diagnoses, and possible ways parents can help their children.

Gardner, R. *MBD: Family Book of Minimal Brain Damage.* New York: Jacob Arson, 1973.

An informative book about MBD for parents and children to share. Dr. Gardner, a psychiatrist, explains the causes of MBD and shows how children may cope with their problems.

Gersh, M. J. *How to Raise Children at Home in Your Spare Time.* Greenwich, Conn.: Fawcett, 1969.

The author tells parents how they can bring up their children well and still keep the fun in their lives. Dr. Gersh is a pediatrician and father of two youngsters. A humorous book with a serious undertone.

Ginott, H.G. *Between Parent and Child.* New York: Avon Books, 1969.

This book was written for parents of all children—to help them live

together more easily. It is a practical guide, with suggestions for han-
dling the conflicts that arise in every family. The author stresses com-
munication between parent and child.

Goldberg, H.K., and G.B. Schiffman, *Dyslexia: Problems of Reading Disabilities.* New York: Grune & Stratton, 1972.

A text that relates the medical and educational aspects of children's reading problems. Although dealt with from a medical point of view, the book is readable and contains valuable information.

Gordon, T. *P.E.T.: Parent Effectiveness Training.* New York: New American Library, 1970.

This book offers guidance for all families in settling conflicts and strengthening relationships. The ideas and methods of P.E.T. are explained, with many examples of successful problem-solving.

Gordon, S. *Living Fully: A Guide for Young People with a Handicap, Their Parents, Their Teachers and Professionals.* New York: John Day, 1975.

Addressed to young people, this book offers practical and relevant information about everyday problems young adults with learning disabilities have. Parents and teachers, too, will find good advice and support in this book.

Handel, R.D., and M. Spiegelman. *The Reader in the Kitchen.* Ridge-field, N.J.: Educational Performance Associates, 1976.

An activity book for parents and children. The authors connect reading with daily experiences at home, using routine household tasks and materials.

Hartman, H. *Let's Play and Learn.* New York: Human Sciences Press, 1976.

This book contains many activities leading to reading and writing skills for youngsters without problems. Most of the suggestions are included in the kindergarten curriculum.

Honig, A. *Parent Involvement in Early Childhood Education.* Washington, D.C.: National Association for the Education of Young Children, 1975.

Mentions a variety of programs that work toward a more active involvement of the family with young children's learning. Current research, the rights of parents, and a list of materials is included.

Kephart, N. *The Slow Learner in the Classroom.* Columbus, Ohio: Charles E. Merrill, 1960.

Primarily for teachers, this book describes one approach to the treatment of learning disabilities in school. Found in most curriculum libraries, this book is representative of theories of perceptual-motor learning.

Kronick, D. *A Word or Two about Learning Disabilities.* San Rafael, Calif.: Academic Therapy Publications, 1973.

The author describes the multiplicity of dysfunctions that vary from child to child and the problems faced by learning-disabled youngsters. She also counsels parents on finding appropriate help for their children.

————, with contributions by others. *What About Me? The LD Adolescent.* San Rafael, Calif.: Academic Therapy Publications, 1975.

This book helps parents and teachers understand the ways in which learning disabilities affect and interfere with a youngster's development. Case histories illustrate problems and hopeful directions.

Lerner, J. *Children with Learning Disabilities.* Boston: Houghton Mifflin, 1971.

A basic textbook presenting theories of diagnosis and strategies for teaching. It gives an overview of the field, primarily for educators, without attempting to promote any single method or theory.

Levy, H. B. *Square Pegs, Round Holes: The Learning-Disabled Child in the Classroom and at Home.* Boston: Little, Brown, 1973.

Addressed to parents and teachers, this book discusses the behavioral as well as the physiological aspects of minimal brain dysfunction. The author believes in the team approach—teacher, parent, and physician.

Murphy, J.F. *Listening, Language and Learning Disabilities: A Guide for Parents and Teachers.* Cambridge, Mass.: Educators Publishing Service, 1970.

This book includes facts about speech and language development as it relates to learning disabilities. The issue of how parent and teacher can help children listen more effectively is also discussed.

Rosenthal, R., and L. Jacobson. *Pygmalion in the Classroom.* New York: Holt, Rinehart & Winston, 1968.

Rosner, J. *Helping Children Overcome Learning Disabilities.* New York: Walker & Company, 1977.

The author talks about how to spot early indications of perceptual problems and how to choose an appropriate remedial approach. Suggested activities for learning, perceptually oriented, are given.

Ross, A.O. *Learning Disabilities: The Unrealized Potential.* New York: McGraw-Hill, 1977.

This book reviews the history of learning disabilities, testing procedures, research in the field, and what can be done for the LD child. The author believes in a behavioral approach.

Siegel, E., *Helping the Brain Injured Child.* New York: Association for Brain Injured Children, 1962.

> *A well-written book for parents of children with learning problems, despite its title. The author describes common experiences and gives suggestions for helping children and their families.*

————. *The Exceptional Child Grows Up.* New York: E.P. Dutton, 1974.

> *The author suggests guidelines for bringing out the maximum potential of each young person by handling specific problems in the environment, parental attitudes, and the child himself. Social, psychological, and vocational goals are discussed.*

Smith, B.K. *Your Nonlearning Child: His World of Upside Down.* Boston: Beacon Press, 1968.

> *The author familiarizes parents and teachers with the world as perceived by children with a variety of problems affecting their learning; emotional disturbance, retardation, perceptuual disabilities. Practical suggestions are offered.*

Stewart, M., and S. Olds. *Raising a Hyperactive Child.* New York: Harper & Row, 1973.

> *A comprehensive discussion of hyperactivity, this book also tells where to find sources of help. The author discusses the use of drugs and gives parents practical suggestions for helping his or her child at home and at school.*

Wagner, R. *Dyslexia and Your Child.* New York: Harper & Row, 1971.

> *This book outlines how parents and teachers can help children learn to read. The author tells how to assess dyslexia at various levels of development and provides definitions of terms.*

Weiss, H.G., and M.S. Weiss. *Home Is a Learning Place.* Boston: Little, Brown, 1976.

> *The authors discuss learning disabilities from their experience as parents of youngsters with learning disabilities. The book offers concrete suggestions for parents to simplify life at home for all the family.*

Wender, P.H. *The Hyperactive Child: A Handbook for Parents.* New York: Crown Publishers, 1973

> *Written for parents, this book deals with the causes, characteristics, and treatment of the hyperactive child. The author advises parents to develop techniques that will minimize the social problems of affected youngsters.*

Pamphlets

Golick, M. "A Parent's Guide to Learning Problems." Quebec Association for Children with Learning Disabilities, 6338 Victoria Avenue, Montreal 252, Quebec, Canada 1970 ($1.00)
The author presents questions and answers that are very basic in this small pamphlet written for parents. It is simply written and informative.
Minde, K., "A Parent's Guide to Hyperactivity in Children." Quebec Association for Children with Learning Disabilities, 6338 Victoria Avenue, Montreal 252, Quebec, Canada ($1.00)
The author describes hyperactivity and discusses the when, why, and how of that condition. She also reviews the main difficulties of the hyperactive child and shows how parents might help.
Silva, W. "The School Daze of the Learning Disability Child." Alpern Communications, 220 Gulph Hills Road, Radnor, Pa. 19087 ($1.00)
A resource and information booklet for parents of children with learning disabilities. It answers some very basic questions for the uninitiated.
Strother, C., R. Hagin, M. Griffen, and L. Letinen-Rogan. *The Adolescent with Learning Disabilities.* San Rafael, Calif.: Academic Therapy Publications, 1975.
Who is the adolescent with learning disabilities, how he feels and how he can be taught are topics dealt with in this small book. Though written for educators, it contains much that will be of interest to parents.
Directory of Facilities for the Learning Disabled and Handicapped. C. Ellingson and J. Cass. Harper & Row, 10 East 53rd St., New York, N.Y. 10022 (1972).
Lists and describes diagnostic facilities serving children and adults in the United States and Canada. Includes information on remedial, therapeutic, and developmental programs.
The Academic Underachiever. Porter Sargent, Publisher, 11 Beacon St., Boston, Mass. 02108 (1971).
A guide to tutorial, remedial, diagnostic, and academic resources in prep-school programs and clinics.
Directory of Summer Camps for Children with Learning Disabilities. Association for Children with Learning Disabilities, 5225 Grace St., Pittsburgh, Pa. 15236 (1974).

Lists and gives basic information on residential summer camps with specialized programs for learning-disabled youngsters and, in some instances, children with other impairments.

A National Directory of Four-Year Colleges, Two-Year Colleges, and Post–High School Training Programs for Young People with Learning Disabilities. P.M. Fielding, ed., Dr. J.M. Moss, directory consultant. Partners in Publishing Company, P.O. Box 50347, Tulsa, Okla. 74150 (1975).

A brief listing of information about opportunities for post–secondary school education of learning-disabled students. Like other somewhat costly directories, this is a resource a local parent organization may want to purchase for sharing among members. Additions and corrections are published in a newsletter, P.I.P., distributed by the publisher. For more information on higher education for learning-disabled young adults, you can also check with local community colleges.

The Hyperactive Child: A Selected Bibliography for Parents and Educators. Current Bibliography Series, P.O. Box 2709, San Diego, Calif. 92112 (1974).

Perceptions. P.O. Box 142, Milburn, N.J. 07041.

A newsletter for parents of children with learning disabilities.

Journals

Learning Disability Quarterly. Dr. Donald D. Deshler, Department of Special Education, 435 Herberrt C. Miller Building, University of Kansas Medical Center, 39th and Rainbow Blvd., Kansas City, Kan. 66103.

Journal of Learning Disabilities. Professional Press, 5 N. Wabash Avenue, Chicago, Ill. 60602.

The Exceptional Parent. Room 708 Statler Office Bldg., 20 Providence Street, Boston, Mass. 02116.

Recordings

Available to learning-disabled students through the Library of Congress, Division of Blind and Disabled, 1291 Taylor Street N.W., Washington, D.C. 20542

Appendices

Definition of Learning Disabilities

The U.S. Office of Education uses the following definition of learning disabilities as a national guideline in allocating funds for the education of the handicapped: "Children with special learning disabilities exhibit a disorder in one or more of the basic psychological processes involved in understanding or in using spoken or written language. These may be manifested in disorders of listening, thinking, talking, reading, writing, spelling, or arithmetic. They include conditions which have been referred to as perceptual handicap, brain injury, minimal brain dysfunction, dyslexia, developmental aphasia, etc. They do not include learning problems which are due primarily to visual, hearing or motor handicaps, to mental retardation, emotional disturbance, or to environmental disadvantage."

UNION FREE SCHOOL DISTRICT

Individual Educational Plan

Date: September 1977

Student Name Teddy Brown Grade 2 Age 7-1 DOB 8/4/70 School
Special Program Resource Room Teacher's Name Miss Robins
Period of IEP September 1977 to June 1978

Annual Goals:

Reading: Teddy will recognize letters and begin to apply phonics skills in decoding words.

Spelling: Teddy will recognize sounds and begin to apply phonics skills in spelling simple words.

Math: Teddy will compute the sum of two numbers under ten.

Specific Special Ed Services Provided and Amount of Time Assigned:

Resource room · 5 x 45 minute sessions per week

Time in Regular Ed Program:

All other time

Signature of Participants
_____
_____
_____

Distribution: White--Special Education Office; Yellow--Teacher; Pink--Parent   (See Second Page for Short Term Objectives)

UNION FREE SCHOOL DISTRICT

Student Name Teddy Brown

Areas	Short Term Instructional Objectives	Current Level of Functioning	Evaluation Procedures	Check When Objective is Achieved
Reading	Teddy will recognize the following consonant blends: st, pl, sl	Teddy can recognize all initial consonant sounds	Teacher-made assessment.	12/77
	Teddy will recognize the following consonant digraphs: sh, ch, th.	Teddy can recognize the "th" digraph some of the time.	teacher-made assessment.	11/77
	Teddy will recognize the short vowel sounds of o, u, e	Teddy can recognize the short sounds of a, i.	weekly test in class.	11/77
Spelling	Teddy will spell correctly cvc trigrams	Teddy can identify the beginning consonant in simple cvc trigrams.	teacher assessment	12/77
Math	Teddy will know addition facts from 1-10 and subtraction facts 1-10.	Teddy can add correctly a number plus one. He has greater difficulty reversing to subtract. Continue to use concrete materials.	teacher assessment	11/77

Organizations and Resources for Information

Academic Therapy Publications
San Rafael, Calif. 94901
In addition to offering a vast listing of reading materials, they will send a few directories listing camps, schools, and clinics upon request. Ask for the Annual Directory of Facilities for the Learning Disabled.

American Speech and Hearing Association
9030 Old Georgetown Road
Washington, D.C. 20014
Leaflets and papers are available on such topics as recognition of communication disorders, hearing impairment and the audiologist, and the speech and language pathologist. Material for parents and professionals.

Association for Children with Learning Disabilities
(ACLD)
2200 Brownsville Road
Pittsburgh, Pa. 15210
A nonprofit federated organization of parents and professionals with state and local affiliates throughout the U.S.A. It is devoted to the well-being and the education of children with learning disabilities and will respond to requests for information on any related topic. State chapters are listed below.

California Association for Neurologically Handicapped Children (CANHC)
Literature Distribution Center
P.O. Box 790
Lomita, Calif. 90717

A good resource with a wealth of printed materials for parents. A listing of pamphlets, papers, and books is available upon request.

Council for Exceptional Children
1411 S. Jefferson Davis Highway
Arlington, Va. 22202

1920 Association Drive
Reston, Va. 22091

A private agency concerned with intellectually gifted as well as handicapped children. The information center responds to requests for information from parents and professionals. It also publishes journals giving valuable information about learning disabilities and other handicapping conditions.

Massachusetts Association for Children with Learning Disabilities
1296 Worcester Road
Box 908
Framingham, Mass.

This group publishes a newsletter of interest to parents and professionals about current issues in the field, legislation, conferences, and research findings. Among other items of interest to parents is a list of colleges (not limited to Massachusetts) that do not have foreign language requirements for admission.

National Information Center for the Handicapped
Closer Look
P.O. Box 1492
Washington, D.C. 20003

Information is available upon request on a variety of issues, including educational and legislative questions pertaining to local areas. It they cannot supply the specific material asked for, they will advise parents and professionals where to find it.

The Orton Society
8415 Bellona Lane
Towson, Md. 21204

A national organization concerned with the problem of specific language disabilities. Publications include books and papers dealing with recognition and remediation of dyslexia. This organization also sponsors conferences throughout the country, of interest to parents and professionals.

Diagnostic Tests

Some of the tests most frequently used by professionals in the course of a diagnostic evaluation are described below. Although the specific materials selected may vary with the examiner and the symptoms and age of the child, some assessment will probably be made in most of the categories. While the list is far from complete, it represents a sampling of materials used. At best, test results are tentative and only reliable in the hands of qualified professionals.

Language Tests

Illinois Test of Psycholinguistics (ITPA) (ages 2.6–10)
   A test yielding a child's psycholinguistic age. Subtests include tasks of auditory, visual, and verbal understanding, association, and expression.
Peabody Picture Vocabulary Test (ages 2.5–18)
   The child selects one of four pictures which depicts the stimulus word presented by the examiner. The test yields a Mental Age and an IQ on the basis of the child's receptive language.
Northwestern Syntax Test (ages 2–8)
   This test screens a child's receptive and expressive knowledge of syntax. Children select the correct sentence in response to a stimulus picture.
Slingerland Screening Tests for Identifying Children with Specific Language Disability (grades 1–8)
   A group test evaluating children's visual, auditory, and motor processing. Perception and memory are also assessed in each modality.

Tests of Intelligence

Wechsler Intelligence Scale for Children-Revised (WISC-R) (ages 5–16)

Perhaps the most widely used of the IQ tests for school-age children, this test consists of two parts, a Verbal Scale, tapping language and verbal abilities, and a Performance Scale, with subtests of perceptual and manipulative tasks. Yields an IQ score for each part of the test as well as a total score.

Wechsler Preschool and Primary Scale of Intelligence (ages 4–6) (WPPSI)

An intelligence scale to appraise the abilities of the preschool child. The test yields an IQ similar to the WISC-R, based on subtests on the Verbal and Performance Scales.

Wechsler Adult Intelligence Scale (ages 16–75 +) (WAIS)

An individual examination for the measurement of adult abilities. Similar to the WISC-R in subtests and form.

Goodenough-Harris Drawing Test

A nonverbal intelligence test scored on the basis of the child's drawing of a human figure.

Stamford-Binet Intelligence Scale (ages 2–18)

An individually administered IQ test, based on age scales. Used primarily for younger children today, it emphasizes verbal skills.

Raven's Coloured Progressive Matrices, (ages 5–11 1/2)

A nonverbal test, the child is asked to select a pattern that would complete a design. It is an ability test of perceptual matching and reasoning, useful for children with language difficulties.

Tests of Motor Development

Lincoln-Oseretsky Motor Development Scale (ages 6–14)
   Assesses the physical development and coordination of children.
   There are age norms for various stages of accomplishments in manual
   ability and motor equilibrium.
The Meeting Street School Screening Test (for kindergarteners and first
graders)
   One of the three parts to this test, the Motor Patterning Subtest
   surveys bilateral sequential movement patterns and awareness of the
   body in space. The other two parts to the test evaluate a youngster's
   visual perception and language abilities.

Tests of Visual Perception

Bender Visual Motor Gestalt Test (ages 6–)
   The child reproduces designs on paper. How he conceives and re-
   produces the forms is interpreted in terms of perception, organiza-
   tion, and emotional indicators.
Beery-Buktenica Developmental Test of Visual-Motor Integration (2–
15)
   The child copies geometric forms, which are then interpreted accord-
   ing to accuracy of reproduction.
Benton Visual Retention Test (8 and up)
   This test assesses children's skill in reproducing designs after the
   forms have been exposed and removed.
The Frostig Developmental Test of Visual Perception (ages 4–9)
   Includes tests of five aspects of visual perception.

Tests of Auditory Perception

Roswell Chall Blending Test
A brief test evaluating a child's ability to blend word parts heard separately into a recognizable word.

Wepman Tests of Auditory Discrimination (5–9)
This is the most frequently used test of discrimination. Word pairs are presented and the child determines if they are the same or different.

WPPSI (Sentences) and WISC (Digit Span)
Children are asked to repeat sentences or numbers in sequence. These subtests measure auditory recall of meaningful and rote material.

Tests of Lateral Dominance

Harris Tests of Lateral Dominance
Used in screening for developmental immaturity of lags with respect to handedness, eyedness, side of the body favored.

Achievement Tests

The Wide Range Achievement Tests (kindergarten–college, 5–adult)
The three subtests cover the academic areas of oral reading, spelling, and arithmetic computation. It is a paper-and-pencil test for spelling and arithmetic. Grade scores are yielded.

Metropolitan Achievement Tests (grades 1–8)
This is an example of the group tests used primarily by schools to assess children's level of achievement in a broad range of language and arithmetic skills.

Reading Tests

Durrell Analysis of Reading Difficulty (grades 2–8)
This test diagnoses reading disabilities at three levels—pre-primary, primary, and intermediate grade levels. Oral reading, silent reading, and listening comprehension are covered.

Gray Oral Reading Tests (grades 1–8)
Children read oral passages in timed situations and answer oral comprehension questions. A grade score results.

Gates-McKillop Reading Diagnostic Tests (grades 2–6)
A diagnostic test of reading skills, including sight vocabulary, phonetic relationships, oral paragraphs, and spelling. Grade scores result for each subtest, as well as qualitative analysis.

Gates-MacGinitie Silent Reading Tests (Grades 1–12)
A silent reading test, with different forms for grade levels. The test assesses vocabulary and comprehension at the earlier levels, adding speed and accuracy from fourth grade through twelfth.

Spache Diagnostic Reading Scales (Grade 1 and up)
An individually administered battery of tests including word lists, graded reading passages, and phonics tests.

Cooperative English Tests: Reading Comprehension (grades 9–14)
Provides scores for level of comprehension, rate of comprehension, and vocabulary.

Developmental Scales

Gesell Developmental Schedules (preschool)
Designed to evaluate the preschool child in the areas of motor development, adaptive behavior, language development, and social behavior.

McCarthy Developmental Scales (preschool)
A measure of the development of skills appropriate for chronological age.

Vineland Social Maturity Scale (preschool)
This test was designed to measure developmental social competence from infancy to school age.

Projective Material

Thematic Apperception Test (TAT) (ages 6–adult)
A projective test of personality in which one is asked to tell stories in response to pictures, revealing drives and fantasies.
Children's Apperception Test (CAT)
Similar to the TAT, but for younger children. The pictures are of animals rather than humans to which children are asked to respond with a story.
House-Tree-Person Drawings
The child is asked to draw a house, tree, and person in turn, and their productions are interpreted in accordance with established clinical norms. Children's drawings are said to reveal their view of themselves and their world.
Rorschach Technique (preschool to adult)
A projective test of personality, using ink blots, to which the child is asked to respond by telling what he sees.

Colleges, Universities and Post-Secondary School Programs

The following schools will accept learning-disabled students. Many of them make special accommodations both in admissions procedures and in curriculum. The list is only a sampling, far from complete, since more colleges and post-secondary school training programs are developing yearly.

Brandywine Junior College
Concord Pike Campus
P.O. Box 7139
Wilmington, Del. 19803

College of the Ozarks
Clarksville, Ark. 72830

Colorado Mountain College
Glenwood Springs, Col. 81461

Curry College Learning Center
848 Brush Hill Road
Milton, Mass. 02186

Ellen Cushing Junior College
Bryn Mawr, Pa. 19010

Hagerstown Junior College
Hagerstown, Md. 21740

Howard University
Washington, D.C. 20001

Johnson and Wales Business
    College
Abbott Park Place
Providence, R.I. 02903

Kingsborough Community
    College
Department of Student Services
2001 Oriental Boulevard
Brooklyn, N.Y. 11235
Attn: Dr. Irwin Rosenthal, CSDC
    Project Director

New England Trade Institute of
    Manchester, New Hampshire
359 Franklin Street
Manchester, N.H. 03101

Oklahoma University
Norman, Okla. 73069
Attn: Department of Vocational
    Rehabilitation

The Para-Educator Center at
N.Y.U.
School of Education, Health,
    Nursing and Arts Profession
New York University
1 Washington Place
New York, N.Y. 10003
*A select number of college-age
young adults are trained to be
para-teachers of nursery school
education.*

Southern Vermont College

Southwestern University

Georgetown, Tex. 78626
Attn: Dr. B. Fullingham, PLUS

University of Michigan at
    Dearborn
4901 Evergreen Road
Dearborn, Mich. 48128

Washington International
    Institute
1740 N Street, N.W.
Washington, D.C.

Westminster College
Fulton, Mo. 65251

Planning Your Child's Education: You Belong on the Team! *

Dos and Don'ts for Parents

At the beginning of this school year, some extremely important things happened which have strengthened the rights of handicapped children—and their parents.

• Final federal regulations were issued, spelling out clearly how the Education for All Handicapped Children Act (Public Law 94–142) will actually work. The regulations were published in August and went into effect October 1. They reinforce our national commitment to a free, appropriate education for every handicapped child, including the most severely disabled. And they set up detailed procedures for achieving that goal.

• Earlier in the year, in April, the federal government took action to enforce the rights of all handicapped people by setting down strong regulations for Section 504 of the Rehabilitation Act of 1973. These regulations assure equal opportunities for the handicapped in every facet of community life; in the area of education, they make clear that no handicapped child may be excluded from publicly supported schooling; that schools (including post-secondary and vocational schools) must be accessible to all; that education must meet individual needs. If a school system persists in denying the rights of the handicapped, it faces the possibility of loss of federal funding. (Section 504 prohibits discrimination against handicapped individuals of all ages by any agency or organization receiving federal funds.)

*This report is reprinted courtesy of Closer Look, the National Information Center for the Handicapped (a Project of the U.S. Department of Health, Education, and Welfare Office of Education, Bureau of Education for the Handicapped, 1978).

Both of these government actions have a direct impact on the lives of handicapped people—an impact which is only beginning to be felt. Both laws, strong and far-reaching as originally written, now have the additional force of specific rules for implementation. There are, some advocates point out, certain ways in which these regulations could have been made even stronger in protecting the rights of the handicapped. But as they stand, they provide new and effective means for bringing handicapped people into the mainstream, at last.

No law is a panacea, and no law can automatically relieve parents and handicapped young people of their frustrations with systems that have only recently begun to include them. The important fact to remember is that opportunities are now available to parents that never existed before. In most cases, it's still going to take hard, persistent work—to make sure that handicapped kids get the education they need. But new opportunities are there—and parents must know how to seize them.

The recognition of the role, and the rights, of parents of handicapped children is one of the most significant changes in public policy brought about by Public Law 94–142. There is no longer any legitimate debate about whether parents should participate in planning and monitoring their child's educational program. Every step along the way—from the time a child's special need is first suspected—a parent's right to take action is now protected by law.

We've put this special issue of our newsletter together *not* to describe each specific regulation of P.L. 94–142, but to help parents use these new legal tools—and sharpen their own skills in fighting for equal opportunities for their children.

We receive letters from parents every day about school programs that are inadequate—or worse. The parents of a ten-year-old daughter born with Down's syndrome write that she was in kindergarten for two years and a "baby-sitting" first grade for the next three because the principal had said "she can't learn anything." A mother writes that she has battled unsuccessfully for thirteen years to get her child, who is diagnosed as having learning disabilities, out of a school "dumping ground." And the father of a teenaged boy writes in agony about years of failure. He asks urgently for some help in finding vocational education so that his son won't drown in his own defeat.

These parents now have the right to demand that their schools do something *at once* about such situations. Programs *must* be reviewed, must take into account each child's individual needs, and must contain specific, appropriate services. Individualized education programs (referred to as IEPs) must be drawn up for every handicapped child—and must be changed as children change.

By law, these programs must be designed by teams including the child's teacher, a school administrator and—you, the parent. *You belong at that conference table.* Your voice in decisions about what happens to your child in school is essential. Your instinct and knowledge about your child are invaluable—and besides, *you* are the one who has the prime responsibility for your child's welfare, not just today, but in the years to come.

This team approach is a new scenario for most people—both parents *and* professionals. We're all going to have to learn a great deal more about working together. There are many school professionals who welcome the idea of conferring with parents as equals, and see the benefits that flow from that relationship. There are others who do not welcome the idea at all, and give it lip service at best. Schools have always been *their* turf, and some of them tend to feel defensive about meetings with parents, as if they were under attack. Often, they see parents as overdemanding and pushy, or apathetic and uncooperative, not realizing that parents frequently are reacting to years of being shoved out of school offices. Many parents, on the other hand, feel shaky about contacts with the school, as if they didn't know enough to hold their own. Others may have become so angry and overbearing that they trigger hostile reactions without even realizing it. New habits of thinking and behaving are needed—not only to make meaningful planning possible, but also to open up lines of communication—so that problems can be dealt with as they come up.

This is a changing school scene, requiring more candor and open discussion, more willingness to face up to our own limitations, to recognize our own biases and see the value of pooling our thoughts and energies. What's wrong, for instance, with administrators admitting openly to parents that they must have more trained teachers and special equipment in order to serve handicapped children adequately—and then going together to the school board or state legislature, to speak up for more funding to create better programs?

It doesn't always work that way. Resistance to change is a reality. There are difficult problems, tragic problems that parents have had to live with for years. And although the law sets up machinery for solving problems through persuasion and understanding, meetings and discussions can break down. To take care of deadlocked situations, a system for settling disputes through impartial hearings is written into the law. This system for protest and appeal is going to require a lot of new learning, too. It can be cumbersome, draining and deeply frustrating.

Unquestionably, parents need help in learning the ropes. Training for parents—not just for teachers—could make things work a lot more smoothly for everyone. Advocacy organizations are taking on this assignment, and courses are springing up in how to get school services under new laws. It's a good idea; in fact, it should be a priority for every parent group. Some parent groups are beginning to set up programs for sensitizing school professionals, administrators, and school board members, too, to the kinds of problems that families of handicapped children must cope with. Efforts like these can change old styles, air old grievances and possibly even bury them . . . so that we can get on with a new, fruitful collaboration between parents and professionals.

Parents are in the decision-making act now, where they belong. It may take some practice—but you can do it! In fact, this is really what hundreds of brave and forceful parents have been doing for years, as they've fought to get their kids out of inferior classrooms, insisted that children who were failing get special teaching, gone doggedly to meeting after meeting to convince schools to accept children who were considered "ineducable."

There's a difference now. A big difference. Now parents have the law on their side. If you and your child have been turned away from school, told "we don't take children like that" or given an exhausting runaround when you tried to get necessary services, this is the time to try again. (And please get the help of an experienced parent or other advocate if you possibly can!)

In the pages that follow, we've tried to be as specific as possible about some of the basic dos and don'ts of parent participation. We hope you'll find these useful. Don't forget . . . the rights of parents are there to protect the rights of children. Learn them . . . and use them!

Due Process in a Nutshell

Throughout this guide, we've indicated times when due process enters the picture. Here's a quick review to keep in mind the main steps involved in due process. Each of these steps reinforces your right to stay on top of decisions about your child.

1. You must receive notice in writing before the school system takes (or recommends) any action that may change your child's school program. Notice in writing is also required if a school refuses to take action to change your child's program.

2. You have the right to give—or withhold—permission for your child to be: tested to determine whether or not he requires special education services (identification); evaluated by specialists to determine what his educational needs are (evaluation); placed in a specific school program to meet his needs (placement).

3. You have the right to see and examine all school records related to the identification, evaluation and placement of your child. If you find that certain records are inaccurate or misleading, you have the right to ask that they be removed from your child's file. Once removed, they may *not* be used in planning for your child's placement.

4. If you do not agree with the school's course of action at *any* point along the way, you have the right to request an impartial due process hearing. This means that you can initiate a hearing to protest any decision related to identification, evaluation or placement of your child.

5. If you fail to win your case, you have the right to appeal the results of the due process hearing to the State Department of Education; and you can appeal to the courts if you lose your case at the state level.

Calling for a due process hearing is your right, but remember that it can be an exhausting process. Before going this route, be sure you have tried to settle differences through every other means—by being as persuasive as possible in meetings with teachers, the principal, special education administrators. If you know that you're up against a brick wall, and you're sure that a due process hearing must be held to resolve conflicting points of view, then you must prepare your case as thoroughly as possible. Be sure to get help from an advocacy group, a lawyer who is familiar with education law and procedures in your state, or an experienced parent. (According to law, the school system must tell you about sources of free or low-cost legal aid. Ask for this information.)

Know your rights at a hearing:

- The hearing officer must be impartial, may not be employed by the school district or be involved in the education of your child.

- You have the right to legal counsel (which includes the advice and support of any advocate, not necessarily a lawyer); to examine witnesses; present evidence; ask questions of school spokespeople; obtain a record of the hearing and all of its findings.

- Write directly to the superintendent of schools in your district to request a hearing. Hearings must be held not later than 45 days after requested. State Departments of Education must review appeals within 30 days.

Laws can seem terribly formidable. It's hard to feel that they really apply to one's own son or daughter. When it comes to figuring out what they mean, our tendency is to leave it all to the "experts."

But we can't. Laws belong to us. You don't have to be a lawyer to understand a law—or to use it to change your life and your child's life.

The following Dos and Don'ts can help you use specific parts of the Education for All Handicapped Children Act that give parents new rights. Each of those parts relates to the ultimate goal of the law: to provide free and appropriate education services for every handicapped child. Each part interconnects with the others like pieces in a puzzle. These important pieces—testing and evaluation, individualized education programs (IEPs), and due process—need you, the parent, to be sure they fit together . . . and work.

None of these procedures is going to work perfectly. There are bugs in every system, and loopholes. Getting appropriate services is still going to be hard work. We hope these pointers will strengthen your hand. Not every one will apply to you; find what fits your situation, and make use of it. Good luck!

If Your Child Has Special Needs, Tell the School about It!

Do . . . Get in touch with your local superintendent of schools without delay if your child has a handicap and is not in school. Your school system is obligated to find all children with disabilities. According to law, no child may be excluded from school because of a handicap. Ask that your child be given an evaluation to find out what kind of program he should have.

The school must take a careful and thorough look at any child who may need special services—by providing a comprehensive evaluation. Once a child is found eligible for special education, the school must arrange to provide appropriate services; a meeting to prepare an individualized education program must be held within 30 days.

Don't forget: all this applies not only to young children, but also to high school age youth with physical, mental and emotional disabilities. They are too often a forgotten population!

Do . . . Find out about preschool services for handicapped children. A great many state laws now call for special programs starting at age three, at least for certain specific disabilities. The principal of your local school (or the district superintendent) can tell you more about available programs. P.L. 94–142 provides incentives for education of children with handicaps between ages three and five, and programs are growing.

Do . . . Make every effort to work with your child's classroom teacher if your child is already in school, but is having problems. There may be some discoveries you and the teacher can make together—things that can be done *right now,* during school hours or after, that can help your child. It will take thought, insight, willingness to try out suggested new activities that can add up to a brighter outlook for your youngster. Some preliminary screening may be done, too, to see if more specialized help is needed at the present time. If problems persist, don't let things slide. If you suspect that your child does have a disability, do go ahead with procedures for getting an evaluation. (Your child's teacher, counselor or principal may carry the ball on this. If not, act on your own.)

Do . . . Remember that you can ask for a reevaluation even if your child is already placed in a special education program. This is especially important if you feel the placement was based on old, inaccurate, or incomplete tests—or if you are dissatisfied with the program. Also, it is important to keep track of a child's needs to make sure that his program continues to be really appropriate, to see if he is ready for a change, or whether his program can be improved.

Do . . . Put your request for an evaluation *in writing*—to the principal of your school or the superintendent. Keep copies of the correspondence. If vital information is discussed on the phone, write a letter confirming the gist of the conversation. Don't trust important matters (like the date, time, and place of an evaluation, or what professionals are in charge of testing your child) to memory.

Due process comes in here. You must receive a written notice from your school system asking your permission to test your child (even if you have requested the evaluation). An explanation of all your rights should be included, including your right to inspect and review all relevant school records about your child.

You must also get a notice in writing if the school turns down your request for evaluation, explaining why. If you can't get an explanation that satisfies you, and you wish to protest this decision, you can request a due process hearing at this point.

Do . . . Keep your own rights file! Use it to document any steps you take to find appropriate education and related services for your child—from the "suspicion of need" stage on up. The file should include: diagnostic test results and other professional reports, your own notations of attempts by you or your child's teacher to solve problems, reports from teachers about your child, copies of letters to and from school officials. Keep copies of state and federal laws and procedures for education of handicapped children and other relevant information. You'll need all this—to keep track of your child's progress, and to stand up for his rights if the school fails to provide an adequate program.

What Should You Know about Testing and Evaluation?

Do . . . Be sure that the evaluation of your child is complete—that it does not consist only of a single test aimed at pinning an IQ score or any other label on him, but is a well-rounded stock-taking by a team of specialists that tells how your child is doing in all areas of his intellectual, physical, and emotional development. This is the only way an appropriate education program can be provided. Information may be gathered in different ways: by talking to people who know your child (including doctors or other professionals), by conferring with classroom teachers, by meeting with you, by observing your child and giving him some tests.

Do . . . Make sure your child has a complete physical examination. This is a must. A child who is thought to be retarded may actually have a visual impairment that has never been discovered. Other difficulties may be caused by hidden physical conditions.

Do . . . Remember—calling a child handicapped by this or that condition does not tell us about his potential, how he learns best, what he can do.

Do . . . Talk about your own observations of your child's behavior, strengths, and weaknesses to members of the evaluation team—to a guidance counselor, or social worker or school nurse. People who do the evaluating must know how a child acts and reacts with different people, in different settings, at different times—in school, on the playground, in his own neighborhood. Your first-hand, round-the-clock knowledge of your child is important information, and should be part of the assessment of your child's needs.

Do . . . Ask what tests will be given to your child, and why. When you sign your name giving permission to have your child tested, make your signature count. Find out what information these tests will yield that can help you and the school know how your child learns; what skills should be strengthened or developed, what problems he has to deal with, what special help he needs. Inform yourself as fully as possible about what these tests are expected to do—before giving your consent to have your child tested. (Tests may be a big mystery area for you, as they are for most people. How about making a study of testing and evaluation through your local parent group or PTA?)

Do . . . Be sure that testing does not discriminate in any way. If a child speaks Spanish or any language other than English, tests must be given in the language he knows best. Children who have grown up in minority cultures should not be judged by answers to questions about a world that is totally strange to them. Children who are deaf must have interpreters; all testing must take the nature of handicaps into consideration, so that the picture of a child's ability is a truly fair one.

Do . . . Insist that the results of testing and evaluation be explained to you in clear, jargon-free terms, and that you have copies for your own file.

Due process comes in here. If you do not feel that the school's evaluation is fair or accurate, you are permitted by law to get an independent evaluation from other professionals. But—you may end up paying for it. The school system can ask for a due process hearing when its evaluation is challenged, to decide whether or not an outside evaluation is neces- sary. If the ruling is in the school's favor, the school does not have to pay. If you do get an independent evaluation (whether or not the school pays for it), it must be considered in decisions about placing your child —and it may be used as evidence in a due process hearing.

Testing will not necessarily mean that your child will be found eligible for special education. If you feel that the school's decision is wrong on this score, you can request a due process hearing at this point.

Get Ready for Meetings to Decide What's Best for Your Child

Do . . . Be sure to attend all meetings held to plan or check into your child's individualized education program (IEP). The law states clearly that an IEP team must include one or both parents, the child's teacher, and a representative of the school system. (Sometimes one or more other specialists may be there, too. If this is the first time your child will get special services, someone who was involved in testing your child must be present.) Schools are expected to make every effort to get in touch with parents to make sure that they come to IEP meetings—and to arrange times that they can come.

IEPs must be prepared for every child who is eligible for special education. If no individualized education program has been drawn up for your child, check into it. This programing is the key to getting appropriate services.

Do . . . Prepare as well as you can for the school meeting that will design your child's educational program. Have your child's file ready, with information easily available on all testing and evaluation that has been done—by the school, or privately. Use your right to go through school records to be sure they are accurate and up-to-date. This meeting must be based on a recent and comprehensive evaluation, so check to be absolutely sure this has happened.

Do . . . Bring along a helper to the IEP meeting, if you will feel more comfortable or secure. More and more people are getting special training to act as advocates for parents in these new and unfamiliar circumstances. Your helper can rehearse with you ahead of time, explain what will go on and how decisions about the IEP will be reached. Ask members of your local parent organization if they are aware of this kind of help. If you can't find someone trained as an advocate, try to get assistance from another parent who has been through it. Experience is a great teacher, and you can benefit from it.

Do . . . Be as clear as possible in your own mind about what kind of things you believe your child is ready to learn. Talk these over with professionals you trust, and rely on your own knowledge of your child, too. Make a checklist of key items. Does your son need to learn to sit still and listen, instead of interrupting constantly or making inappropriate comments? Does your daughter need to learn how to speak distinctly? Does she need help with self-care skills? Is your teenager getting pre-vocational or job-skill training?

Do . . . Be able to back up your requests for special kinds of help with diagnostic reports, observations and other information from professionals who know your child. If you wish, you may ask to have professionals accompany you to support your point of view. This is your right according to law.

Do . . . Remember—diagnostic reports, important as they are, are not infallible. They don't say *all* there is to be said about a child. Your most important job is to make sure that the others at the conference never forget that you're talking about a real child—not scores attained on a series of psychological tests. Bring up all the real-life information you feel is relevant to a discussion about your son or daughter's educational needs. In the past, there was far too much tendency to rely on reports and records, not to look at the child himself. This is your chance to push for this change in perspective.

Do . . . Be wary of any suggestion to place your child (or leave him) in a classroom that has a label. The old approach was to give children "trainable retarded education" or "blind education" or "physically handicapped education," which more often than not meant inferior education, or none at all. That's what the new law is supposed to stop. The program your child gets should be built on services that relate to strengths and abilities, special problems and learning needs . . . not to his category of disability. If you don't agree that this is what the program does, speak up for your point of view—and make sure that changes are made.

Do . . . Try to understand the issue of "mainstreaming" as fully as possible. The law is based on the right of handicapped children to be part of the world, to learn, work and play alongside their nonhandicapped schoolmates. The law's words for it are: educating children in the "least restrictive environment." Somebody coined the word "mainstreaming" to describe this view and the term stuck. Whatever words you use, it makes a big difference in the image that children have of themselves, their confidence and their ability to get along as accepted members of society. This doesn't mean that every handicapped child belongs in a regular class. But he should be given that chance, if, with sufficient aid and understanding, he can hold his own. And if a child spends all day in a separate class because his need for small classes is so great, he should be given every possible opportunity to join his peers in other school activities. This is an essential part of his education.

Do . . . Take some time to think about how to be assertive without "taking over" or antagonizing people. Meetings about a child's school needs are not intended to be hostile confrontations; they should provide the chance for honest examination of alternatives. One way to keep it successful is to realize you do have an essential role to play as an equal-status member of the team—along with educators. Keep calm, listen to what the others have to say, and ask them to extend the same courtesy to you. Your points of view may be new to each other, and you may disagree, but you can learn from one another. If everyone is truly concerned about giving a child the chance he needs to grow and learn, it should be possible to iron out disagreements through persuasion and mutual understanding.

Do . . . Make sure that your child is not excluded from participating in a regular school program because of architectural barriers. This is against the law. Section 504 states very clearly that school facilities must be made accessible and that special adaptations must be made so that services are really available to all students.

Study the Final IEP Before Giving Your Consent—and Insist on Essential Services

Do . . . Have a very complete understanding of the IEP that is produced. A copy of the final IEP should be given to you in writing. Make sure that the education goals that are agreed on are specific and that they accurately reflect decisions that were made at the meeting.

An IEP should not contain general goals, like: "Maximize child's potential," but should include clear-cut objectives that can be measured. One objective, for instance, could be: to be able to identify a specific number of words by sight within a certain period of time. Long-term goals such as reading at a first-grade level should be included, too—so you know where you're going.

An IEP should also say how much time a child is to spend in the mainstream, either in regular classes or extracurricular activities. Services to be given should be clearly defined. For instance, if speech therapy is in the IEP, how often will it take place? What kinds of activities will it include? When will it start? How long will it go on? How will progress be charted? If other supportive services, such as transportation or hearing aids, are needed, this should be in writing, too.

Check the whole thing carefully—with people who can advise you. The better you know and understand the IEP, the better you will be able to follow your child's progress, monitor the program to see if it is effective, and ask for changes or modifications when necessary.

Do . . . Make sure that appropriate vocational education is in your son or daughter's IEP. This has been a terribly neglected area; insist that work-skill training, on-the-job experience, and other skills related to independent living are built into the school program provided for your teenager—as needed. There may not even be a vocational education program for handicapped students in your school system. (You may have to work hard with administrators and teachers to get one started. But speaking up about the need, making sure it's in the IEP, is a first step.)

Do . . . Be firm about things you consider important. Although you don't want to be so rigid that no possible plan could ever get off the ground, you are the main protector of your child's interests. If the proposed program segregates your child in a separate classroom all day, and you are convinced that he should have the chance to make it in a regular school activity (at least part of the day), stick to your guns. If a specific classroom or school has been recommended, visit it—to see if it really meets your child's needs. Art, music, school plays, gym, shop are part of the school day for other kids. Your handicapped child should be included. This will require modifications in the way programs are offered —but it can be done!

Due process comes in here. Parents must give their consent to placement of their child. If you feel that an essential part of the program is omitted, is harmful to your child, or is truly inappropriate, you should make your objections known. If the school system is not able to provide the kind of educational program your child must have, it is responsible, by law, for financing an appropriate education in a private facility. This can be a difficult bone of contention, and requires detailed evidence. In all controversies, you must put together documents, reports, letters and other statements (from teachers, doctors, and other specialists who know your child) to support your view. If possible, meet with the school members of the IEP team again to present your side. If you reach a dead end and are unable to convince school officials to change the program or placement, then ask for a due process hearing at this point. While controversial issues are being decided, children must be permitted to remain in their present school setting.

Follow Your Child's Program, Make Sure It's Working

Do . . . Get to know the teacher, once your child is placed. Ask when he or she would like to meet with you. Regular conferences are important—to find out how your child is doing, to bring up questions you have, to discuss any possible new efforts at school or at home. A good, trusting relationship between you and the teacher can catch a lot of problems before they get too big to manage.

Do . . . Help teachers and other people in school learn more about handicaps. You can help overcome feelings of fear and pity that come from lack of experience. Share books and articles. If possible, arrange for your child's teacher to visit with your son or daughter before school starts (or after school some day) so he or she has a chance to get a feeling for your child's personal qualities. (The extra boost to their relationship will help them both survive later problems—if they arise.) Offer to talk to other parents in the class—so they in turn can help their children accept and understand differences . . . and make friends. You want your child to become independent—but it won't help him to have to deal with unnecessary fear or aggression based on ignorance.

Do . . . Make sure that a formal evaluation of your child's program takes place every year . . . at the very least. If you stay in close touch with the classroom teacher (and other specialists who work with your child), you'll be able to know if changes should take place sooner—and will certainly be able to play a more meaningful part in planning next steps. Making sure that a program continues to be appropriate requires vigilant checking and rechecking . . . to see if school placement is actually encouraging a child's growth.

Do . . . Listen to your child, respect what he's saying. You need to know his reaction to schoolwork, to teachers, to classmates. He may need help getting "toughened up" in the real school world. If you are worried about how things are going . . . again, talk to the teacher, or the school counselor or principal, for advice and suggestions. Keep all your lines of communication open.

But Please

Don't . . . let other people plan for you. If, for instance, you have reason to think that school people met "behind the scenes" to agree on the IEP, effectively keeping you out of the act, you have grounds to complain loudly. Some school administrators have had nothing but difficult experiences with parents and freeze at the thought of working with them. (It works the other way around, too. You may have had so many frustrating or intimidating experiences that you don't want to try again. Please do.) You and the school can work together. Don't let the potential for a new creative process die by default.

Don't . . . settle for poor or inadequate services. If you find that your child's problems are ignored, that special resource teachers or educational materials don't exist, that your child is deprived of assistance he needs to adjust to a mainstreamed classroom in which he has been placed—take action. Demand changes in keeping with the promise of an appropriate program.

Due process comes in here. If your efforts to work with your child's teacher, principal, or school administrators fail, you have a right to request a due process hearing at this point in order to protest your child's placement.

Don't . . . let yourself feel put down at the meetings held to discuss, plan or evaluate your child's program. It may sound scary at first, but it really doesn't have to be. When professionals use language you don't understand, feel free to ask for explanations. Remember that you are all there for the same purpose: to work out what's best for your child—to pinpoint his needs and to make decisions on what resources, services, and special programs he needs in order to learn. You can make a valuable contribution by raising questions when ideas and recommendations don't seem to make sense.

Don't . . . forget that, no matter how important every educational service provided to your child may be, he is a young, responsive, growing individual, with human needs to laugh, play, make friends—not a composite of diagnosed needs. The brightness of social success means as much as academic progress (sometimes it can mean even more). This side of life can be overlooked in conscientious efforts to improve learning skills. Your handicapped child is a person—and the purpose of all these efforts is to help him use his own strengths to become the most fulfilled person he can be. That's why it's so important to give each kid as much chance as possible to join the mainstream and to be part of the fun activities of school.

Don't . . . try to do this all alone. Join with other parents in an organization for handicapped individuals, or the PTA, to learn all you can about new federal and state laws, the way your own school system works, how to stick up for your rights. There's so much to do! You're not the only one who needs help. Find your allies—and work together. If teaching programs for handicapped children are below standard, and none of your efforts to bring about improvement have worked, you will be far more effective if you become part of an organized group. You can add strength to a broader effort to implement and strengthen existing laws, to push for increased funding by state legislatures, to awaken the rest of the community to the rights of handicapped children.

Facts about Income Taxes

An Information Sheet on 1977 Federal Income Tax Deductions for Handicapped Persons and Their Parents

A major change in the 1977 tax law is that the former standard deduction has been replaced by a flat amount the law calls the "zero bracket amount." The amount depends on your filing status. The new zero bracket amounts, like deductions, are not taxed. They are: $3,200 of income if you are a married person filing a joint return or a qualifying widow(er); $12,200 of income if you are a single person or an unmarried head of household; or $1,600 of income if you are married filing separately. They are built into the tax tables (used by most taxpayers).

If you are a parent of a handicapped person you have several possibilities for claiming deductions and/or tax credits in addition to the zero bracket amounts:

I. EXEMPTIONS:

You can claim the $750 dependent exemption deduction for your child if he received more than half his support from you and had less than $750 gross income during the year. If the child is under nineteen or if he is a full-time student (regardless of age) in an educational institution, the $750 income limitation does not apply.

What to include in "support":

In figuring out whether or not you contribute to more than half his support, use actual expenses. You can include board, clothing, education, vacations, medical and dental care, medical care insurance premiums, entertainment, and so forth. Keep reasonable records to document such expenses. You can include lodging, too, using its fair market value for your calculations. Capital items such as furniture, appliances, and automobiles, if they are in fact for the individual in question, may be included in figuring the total. If your son or daughter receives social security benefits as the child of a deceased or disabled parent, or Supplemental Security Income, although not taxable, they do count in determining support as his or her share and must be compared to the amount which you as the parent contribute in computing who provides more than half of the support.

If your child is in a public institution or a private residential school:

Even if you pay less than half or none of the cost of tuition, room and board, you can claim him as a dependent regardless of his age and take the exemption deduction of $750 if the facility can qualify as an "educational institution." In such a case, tuition, room and board is considered a scholarship and need not enter into your support calculations. (The institution must be making an effort to educate or train the person to use his faculties to the extent that he is physically or mentally able to do so.)

The Internal Revenue Service provides a worksheet (Form 2038) for calculating support.

II. MEDICAL DEDUCTIONS:

In deciding whether or not you can consider your handicapped family member a dependent for purposes of medical deductions (as distinguished from exemption deductions) you can include any family member, regardless of age, and even if he has an income of more than $750 per year, *as long as you furnished more than half the person's support during the year.*

That part of your total medical expenses paid during the year which exceeds 3 percent of your adjusted gross income can be deducted. Expenses for "medical care" include any amounts paid for the "diagnosis, cure, mitigation, treatment, or prevention" of a disease or a handicapping condition or "for the purpose of affecting the structure or function of the body." Such expenses can include:

1. Fees paid to physicians, dentists, optometrists, psychologists, psychiatrists, registered nurses, practical nurses, therapists, hospitals, or laboratories. Drugs and medicines are deductible too, but you can include only what exceeds 1 percent of your adjusted gross income. Contraceptives, over-the-counter medicines, vitamins, and special foods or beverages, if prescribed by a doctor, are deductible. The foods and beverages must be in addition to, not a substitute for, foods normally eaten by the dependent.

2. The entire cost of a residential school or institution, of a special day school, of a special class within a regular school, of a special class within a parochial school, of a sheltered workshop, special camp, or

other special schooling, including the cost of meals if provided, *if the principal purpose of the class, school, camp or institution is to mitigate or treat the dependent's handicapping condition.* The expense of a special community residence such as a halfway house or group home, is deductible, too, under the same restraints.

3. Transportation expenses (a) essential for obtaining "medical care" (diagnosis, cure, mitigation, treatment or prevention of a handicapping condition); (b) incurred in visiting a dependent at a residential facility if the taxpayer's medical advisors consider the visits a necessary part of the dependent's treatment. You can also deduct the cost of hiring a person to accompany a handicapped child who cannot travel alone to obtain "medical care" as described above. Costs of meals and lodgings on long trips to get medical care, including trips to take a handicapped dependent to a special school, institution or camp, are deductible too.

Transportation expenses would include plane, train, bus or taxi fares. (Be sure to keep proof of expenditures.) If you go by car, IRS allows 7¢ per mile, parking fees, and tolls. If you prefer, you can deduct gas and oil costs instead of 7¢ per mile.

4. The entire expense of a registered or licensed nurse can be deducted. Costs of practical nurses, domestic helpers, or companions who give direct services to the disabled person are deductible too, but only that part of the wages that covers time spent in actual care of the handicapped person. If the caregiver's board is paid by the taxpayer, that is deductible too.

5. Other special medical deductions:

(a) Medical Insurance Premiums: One-half of medical insurance premiums paid by you are deductible, up to $150 without regard to the 3 percent limitation. The rest of your medical insurance premiums are also deductible, but as an ordinary medical expense —i.e., subject to the 3 percent limitation.

(b) Costs of special equipment (including installation) to alleviate the person's handicap, but it must be depreciated over its useful life if its use extends beyond the tax year; eyeglasses, crutches, braces, wheelchairs, incontinent pants and pampers if the child is well beyond the age of normal continence, artificial limbs and teeth, hearing aids, tape recorders, special mattresses, guide dogs (and upkeep), elevators, air conditioning if considered essential by a physician to alleviate the handicap, special equipment in automobiles, and the like. If the special equipment does not improve the value of your property, you can deduct the total cost; if it does, you can deduct the difference between the cost and the improvement in value.

III. TAX CREDITS:

1. *General Credit:*

For 1977 the general tax credit is taken into consideration in the tax tables. So if you use the tax tables, you do not compute the general tax credit. But if you don't use the tax tables, you are allowed to compute your general tax credit. Credits differ from deductions. Deductions are subtracted from your income before a tax figure is determined. Credits are subtracted not from income, but from the amount of tax. Thus, subtracting credits is the final step in determining the tax owed. Unless you are married and filing separately, to determine the amount of your general credit, choose whichever amount is greater—(a) $35 for each person you are entitled to claim as a dependent, or (b) 2 percent of your tax table income reduced by the zero bracket amount. The credit computed in this way cannot exceed $180. If you are married, filing separately, and do not use the tax tables, your general tax credit is $35 for each exemption claimed. If the general credit brings the amount owed below $0, the government will not owe you—that is, no refund or carryover is allowed.

2. *Child Care Credit:*

The tax law again allows a tax credit for child care or disabled dependent care expenses necessary to permit the taxpayer to be gainfully employed. Form 2441 should be used to compute this credit and attached to your form 1040. You subtract the total dollar credit due you from your tax bill after all deductions have been figured. If the credit brings the amount owed below 0, the government will not owe you money; no refund or carryover is allowed, just as it is not allowed for the general credit.

To be eligible for this credit you must have a dependent for whom you can claim the dependency exemption under the age of fifteen, or a spouse or dependent of any age who is disabled and incapable of self-care. One such dependent earns the taxpayer a credit of 20 percent of all household and personal care expenses up to $2,000 (or $400). Two or more earn a credit of 20 percent of care expenses up to $4,000 (or $800 maximum credit).

Expenses must be employment related. That is, they must have been incurred to enable the taxpayer and his or her spouse, if married, *to work full-time or part-time,* or *to be a full-time student.* And the expenses must go toward assuring the well-being and protection of the dependent or disabled child or adult.

Married couples (living together) must file a joint return in order to claim the credit. Both the parents must be gainfully employed, but gainful employment as defined above includes being a part-time worker or a full-time student at an educational institution during five months of the tax year. If one spouse is a part-time worker, child care expenses allowable towards the credit cannot be greater than the earnings of the person with the lower income. If one spouse is a full-time student, he is treated as if he earned $166 per month (with one dependent) or $333 per month (with two or more dependents).

Single taxpayers who work part-time or who are full-time students are eligible under the same conditions and restraints. A divorced or legally separated parent is considered a single taxpayer. (See IRS Publication #503.)

Employment-related expenses may include:

Household services performed in or about the home as necessary, if incurred for the well-being and protection of the dependent child or disabled adult. The services of housekeepers, maids, or cooks are ordinarily considered necessary. Gardeners are not. The employer's share of FICA (social security) taxes paid in connection with the wages should be included in the total wages paid for household and dependent care. Meals and lodging furnished to a housekeeper are deductible too.

Payments for care of a child under age fifteen can be applied to the credit whether the payments are for care in the home or out of the home (e.g., in a baby sitter's home, a day-care center, or a preschool). The care of an older disabled dependent must take place within the person's own home to qualify for the credit. Child care payments to a relative can be counted towards the credit only if the relative is not a dependent of the taxpayer and if the taxpayer files FICA tax form 942.

Note: Some disabled dependent care expenses may qualify as employment-related and also as medical expenses. These may not be included in both computations.

3. *Earned Income Credit:*

There is a tax benefit offered to persons whose earned income or adjusted gross income (whichever is larger) is less than $8,000.

To be eligible you must:

(a) Maintain a household for the entire year as the main place of residence for you and your child who is under nineteen years of age or a student, whether or not you are entitled to claim him as a dependent, or a disabled child over nineteen, not a full-time student, who is a dependent. The definition of "child" includes adopted children, stepchildren, and *foster children* who live with you for the entire tax year. (See IRS Publication #17, p. 152 for certain other provisions.)

(b) Have a taxable year that represents a full twelve months.

(c) File a joint return if you are married.

To compute the credit:

Take 10 percent of the first $4,000 of earned income ($400 maximum). Anything earned over $4,000 must then be reduced by 10 percent of the amount in excess. (Thus if your income is as high as $8,000, the credit would be eliminated.)

Unlike the General Credit and the Child Care Credit, this credit is refundable. That is, if in subtracting the credit from what you owe in taxes you go below $0, the government *will* owe you the amount and will refund it. Thus you should subtract the general and child care credits and reduce your tax as much as possible before subtracting the earned income credit. Also, it is important to know that this credit will not reduce other benefits financed by federal funds (such as Aid to Dependent Children).

A general word of advice: Any deductions or credits you claim will need documentation. Be sure to keep receipts, canceled checks, bills, records of travel, records of dates of payment, amount paid, who provided the services, and briefly what he or she did. And it is important to understand that tax law is sometimes subject to varying interpretations.

The Internal Revenue Service Publication 17, *Your Federal Income Tax, 1978 Edition,* contains complete information about all of the items discussed here. It is available at any IRS office. Or you might want to ask for two specific publications that are very helpful: 502 Deals with *Deductions for Medical and Dental Expenses* and 503 deals with *Child Care and Disabled Dependent Care.* (The information contained in 502 and 503 is also contained in Publication 17.)

ACLD State Chapters

ALABAMA (Alabama ACLD)
President
Mrs. Ronnie Carr
P.O. Box 11588
Montgomery, Ala. 36111
(205) 272-6096

ALASKA (Alaska ACLD)
President
Gloria D. Oakes
7420 Old Harbor Ave.
Anchorage, Alaska 99504
(907) 333-6372

ARIZONA (Arizona ACLD)
President
Mrs. Pat French
5609 Sailor's Reef Rd.
Tempe, Ariz. 85283
(602) 838-6411
State Office
P.O. Box 15525
Phoenix, Ariz. 85060
(602) 248-7373

ARKANSAS (Arkansas ACLD)
President
Mrs. Dolly D. Garrison

Route #7, Box 138
Pine Bluff, Ark. 71603
(501) 879-0057
State Office
P.O. Box 5508
Brady Station
Little Rock, Ark. 72205

CALIFORNIA (CANHC)
President
Mr. Jack Graydon
9126 E. Leroy St.
San Gabriel, Calif. 91775
(213) 287-8778
State Office
P.O. Box 4088
Los Angeles, Calif. 90051
(213) 831-8644

COLORADO (Colorado ACLD)
President
Vernon Lewis
3630 Ivy Street
Denver, Col. 80207
(303) 333-9296
State Office
Russell DeWitt
P.O. Box 55 Loretto Station

Denver, Col. 80236
(303) 934-6956

CONNECTICUT (CACPLD, INC.)
President
Mr. Albert Chamberlin
14 Plainfield Rd.
West Hartford, Conn. 06107
(203) 236-5349
State Office
20 Raymond Rd.
West Hartford, Conn. 06107
(203) 236-3953

DELAWARE (Diamond State ACLD)
President
Mrs. Mary Lou Walsh
R.D. #3, Bridleshire Farms
Newark, Del. 19711
(302) 239-5225
State Office
2400 W. 17th St.
Wilmington, Del. 19806
(302) 571-0230

DISTRICT OF COLUMBIA (District of Columbia ACLD)
President
Suzan Wynne
3915 Livingston St.
Washington, D.C. 20015
(202) 244-6861

FLORIDA (Florida ACLD)
President
Dr. Ronald Cantwell
8330 S.W. 16th St.

Miami, Fla. 33155
(305) 264-5738

GEORGIA (Georgia ACLD)
Co-Presidents
Dr. Elliott McElroy
2294 Lanier Place
Morrow, Ga. 30260
(404) 961-0330
Mrs. Mary Steigerwald
1055 Pine Mountain Dr.
Forest Park, Ga. 30050
(404) 961-5300
State Office
P.O. Box 29492
Atlanta, Ga. 30329
(404) 633-1236

HAWAII (Hawaii ACLD)
President
Mrs. Phyllis Rice
2877 Kalakaua 107
Honolulu, Hawaii 96815
State Office
Mrs. Ivalee Sinclair, Executive Director
P.O. Box 4203
Honolulu, Hawaii 96813
Home: (808) 988-4962
Office: (808) 949-4941

IDAHO (Idaho ACLD)
President
Mrs. Barbara Balding
5217 Wylie Lane
Boise, Idaho 83703
(208) 343-8620
State Office
Same address

ILLINOIS (Illinois ACLD)
President
Mrs. Dorothy Ellis
2229 W. Winnebago Rd.
Peoria, Ill. 61614
(309) 691-3484
State Office
P.O. Box A 3239
Chicago, Ill. 60690

INDIANA (Indiana ACLD)
President
Mrs. Ellie Thurston
6417 Dean Rd.
Indianapolis, Ind. 46220
(317) 251-9813
State Office
Same address

IOWA (Iowa ACLD)
President
Lynne Cannon
920 Highwood St.
Iowa City, Iowa 52240
(319) 337-5731
State Office
Same address

KANSAS (Kansas ACLD)
President
Joe D. Swalwell
5507 W. 15th St
Topeka, Kan. 66604
(913) 272-0033
State Office
P.O. Box 4424
Topeka, Kan. 66604

KENTUCKY (Kentucky ACLD)
President
Mr. Oscar M. Marvin
2442 Parkdale Ave.
Louisville, Ky. 40218
State Office
P.O. Box 18016
Louisville, Ky. 40218
(502) 584-6289

LOUISIANA (Louisiana
ACLD)
President
Charles Nolan
7100 St. Charles Ave.
New Orleans, La. 70118
(504) 861-9503
State Office
Same address

MAINE (Maine ACLD)
President
Mrs. Barbara Howd
14 Spencer St.
Orono, Maine 04473
(207) 866-2888
State Office
Same address

MARYLAND (Maryland
ACLD)
President
Mrs. Mary Martinez
3719 36th St.
Mt. Rainier, Md. 20822
(301) 277-4687
State Office

Mrs. Margaret Duffy, Secretary
320 Maryland National Bank
  Building
Baltimore, Md. 21202

MASSACHUSETTS (Mass.
  Child)
Catherine S. McLeod
P.O. Box 261
Chestnut Hill, Mass. 02167
(617) 734-4508
Blue Hills ACLD
Mrs. George Norris
154 West St.
Randolph, Mass. 02368
(617) 963-5407
Hingham ACLD
Mrs. Virginia Kelly
88 Smith Rd.
Hingham, Mass. 02043
(617) 749-2697

MICHIGAN (Michigan ACLD)
President
Judith A. Haught
100 E. Jackson
Lansing, Mich. 48906
(517) 489-5064
State Office
Helene Gruber, Executive
  Secretary
2338 N. Woodward
Royal Oak, Mich. 48073
(313) 548-4455

MINNESOTA (Minnesota
  ACLD)
President
James E. Stoddart

1860 Shadywood Rd.
Wayzata, Minn. 55191
(612) 471-8313
State Office
Mary Jo Richardson, Executive
  Director
1821 University Ave.
St. Paul, Minn. 55104
(612) 646-6136

MISSISSIPPI (Mississippi
  ACLD)
President
Mrs. Betty D'Aquilla
752 E. Railroad Ave.
Long Beach, Miss. 39560
(601) 864-1146
State Office
P.O. Box 12083
Jackson, Miss. 39211
(601) 982-2812

MISSOURI (Missouri
  ACLD)
President
Mrs. Juanita Blevins
1809 E. 125th St.
Kansas City, Mo. 64146
(816) 942-6139
State Office
P.O. Box 3303
Glenstone Station
Springfield, Mo. 65804

MONTANA (Montana ACLD)
President
Mrs. W. L. (Susie) MacBoyle
511 Burlington

Billings, Mont. 59101
(406) 259-9321
State Office
Same address

NEBRASKA (Nebraska
ACLD)
President
Mrs. Viridiann Gorman
1720 N. Taylor
Grand Island, Neb. 68801
(308) 382-8989
State Office
P.O. Box 6464
Omaha, Neb. 68106
(402) 391-8622

NEVADA (Nevada ACLD)
President
Ms. Theresa Smith
4034 S. Great Plains Way
Las Vegas, Nev. 89121
(702) 458-1445
(702) 878-6841

NEW HAMPSHIRE
(New Hampshire
ACLD)
President
Louise Huppe
292 Arah St.
Manchester, N.H. 03104
(603) 623-5820
State Office
Same address

NEW JERSEY (New Jersey
ACLD)

Interim President
Morris I. Pollack
270 Passaic Ave.
Passaic, N.J. 07055
(201) 777-5500
State Office
P.O. Box 249
Convent Station, N.J. 07961
(201) 539-4644

NEW MEXICO (New Mexico
ACLD)
President
Margie McCament
1606 Hermosa N.E.
Albuquerque, N.M. 87110
(505) 265-2217
State Office
Judy Zanotti
American Bank Building, Suite
1119
200 Lomas Blvd. N.W.
Albuquerque, N.M. 87102
(505) 842-8713

NEW YORK (New York ACLD)
President
Vincent Fontana
340 E. 18th St.
Brooklyn, N.Y. 11226
(212) 282-8854
State Office
Mr. Peter Larson, Executive Di-
rector
Richardson Hall
Room 272, SUNY-Albany
Albany, N.Y. 12222
(518) 472-7110

NORTH CAROLINA
(North Carolina
ACLD)
President
Mrs. Margaret Sigmon
68 Willow Terrace
Chapel Hill, N.C. 27514
(919) 929-2286
State Office
Box 2793
Chapel Hill, N.C. 27514

NORTH DAKOTA
(North Dakota
ACLD)
President
Mrs. Judy Podoll
1866 S. Grandview Lane
Bismarck, N.D. 58501
(701) 258-8293
State Office
Same address

OHIO (Ohio ACLD)
President
Charles Ambuske
8110 E. New Carlisle Rd.
New Carlisle, Ohio 45344
(513) 845-1693
State Office
Mrs. Dorothy Doria, Executive
Secretary
333 W. National Rd.
Englewood, Ohio 45322
(513) 836-0415

OKLAHOMA (Oklahoma
ACLD)
President
Mrs. Brenda Finnegan
2609 Whippoorwill
Enid, Okla. 73701
(405) 237-5557
State Office
Janet Hatchett, Secretary
3701 N.W. 62nd St.
Oklahoma City, Okla. 73112
(405) 943-9434

OREGON (Oregon ACLD)
President
Bill Clawson
2222 N.E. 92nd Ave.
Portland, Ore. 97220
State Office
Geneva Winkel, Executive
Director
Special Education Dept.
Portland State University
P.O. Box 751
Portland, Ore. 97207
(503) 229-4439

PENNSYLVANIA (Pennsylvania
ACLD)
President
Mr. Joseph Hart
609 Kennard Rd.
State College, Pa. 16801
(814) 466-7235
State Office
Mrs. Renee Sourber, Secretary
1383 Arcadia Rd.
Lancaster, Pa. 17601

RHODE ISLAND (Rhode Island
ACLD)

President
Mrs. Betty Gallipeau
76 Lincoln Avenue
Barrington, R.I. 02806
(401) 246-1439
State Office
P.O. Box 6685
Providence, R.I. 02904

SOUTH CAROLINA (South Carolina ACLD)
President
Jill E. McGovern, Ph.D.
State Office
The College of Charleston
Charleston, S.C. 29401
(803) 722-0181

SOUTH DAKOTA (South Dakota ACLD)
President
Mrs. Jan Van Veen
1605 So. 10th Ave.
Sioux Falls, S.D. 57105
(605) 339-9640
State Office
Same address

TENNESSEE (tennessee ACLD)
President
Mrs. Jane Wolfe
57 Bethany Dr.
Jackson, Tenn. 38301
(901) 423-0362
State Office
Same address

TEXAS (Texas ACLD)
President
Betty S. DeuPree
209 Hermosa
El Paso, Tex. 79922
(915) 584-4338
State Office
Mary Poplin, Executive Director
1011 W. 31st St.
Austin, Tex. 78705
(512) 458-8234

UTAH (Utah ACLD)
President
Mrs. Lee Zumbrunnen
1896 E. 3780 So.
Salt Lake City, Utah 84106
(801) 277-2870
State Office
Same address

VERMONT (Vermont ACLD)
President
Mrs. Fran Rice
RFD #2
Stowe, Vt.
(802) 253-4256
State Office
9 Heaton St.
Montpelier, Vt. 05602

VIRGINIA (Virginia ACLD)
President
Mrs. Valerie Robinson
3714 Windingway Rd., S.W.
Roanoke, Va. 24015
(703) 343-7912

State Office
June Gray, Secretary
P.O. Box 13410
Richmond, Va. 23225
(804) 320-5166

WASHINGTON (Washington ACLD)

President
Mrs. Barbara Pattison
9319 42nd St. N.E.
Seattle, Wash. 98115
(206) 242-9400
State Office
Mozelle Sims, Director
444 N.E. Ravenna Blvd., Room 206
Seattle, Wash. 98115
(206) 523-9768

WEST VIRGINIA (West Virginia ACLD)

President
Mrs. Kay Crum
P.O. Box 117
Charlton Heights, W.V. 25040
(304) 779-9558
State Office
Same address

WISCONSIN (Wisconsin ACLD)

President
John Westerlund
Rt. 1, Box 112
Washburn, Wis. 54891
(715) 272-2536
State Office
Same address

AFFILIATION ABROAD

Canada
Canadian ACLD
Kildare House
323 Chapel Street
Ottawa, Ontario
K1N 7Z2
(613) 238-5721

Quebec ACLD
4820 Van Horne Avenue, Suite 8
Montreal, Quebec
Canada H3W 1J3

Germany
Family Forum
Mrs. Judith Fontana
86 TFW Box 4304
APO 09009

Index

academic evaluation, 127
academic success, zeal for, 5
acceptance of problem, 27–32
activity level, 20–21
adolescent period, 64–65,
    78–83
  impulsivity, 52–53
  suggestions for parents, 81–83
Ames, Louise, 22, 157
amphetamines, 137
anoxia, 21
anticipation and prevention,
    technique of, 57
anxiety, 31, 42
Association for Children with
    Learning Disabilities
    (ACLD), 128, 151
  list of chapters, 206–213
attention span, 20–21, 62, 96
awareness, of the problem,
    26–27

Barsh, Ray, 134, 158
bed wetting, 85

behavioral manifestations, 7,
    15–17, 41–44, 52, 62, 70,
    72
behavioral psychologists, 44
behavior modification therapy,
    136–37
biochemical factors, 21, 156
birthday parties, 67
Blume, Judy, 67, 157
book report homework, 107–8,
    109
brain injury, 4, 21
Brutten, Dr. Milton, 120, 157
bulletin board, 59

California Association for
    Neurologically Handicapped
    Children, 132
camp, 76
causation and contributing
    factors, 17–25
  activity level and attention
    span, 20–21

brain injury and minimal brain dysfunction (MBD), 21
education, 24–25
emotional problems, 22–23
environment, 23–24
genetic factors, 21–22
immaturity or maturational lag, 22
intelligence, 18
sensory deficits, 19–20
change, fear of, 15–16
Chariot of the Gods, 14, 15
child's future, learning disabilities and, 140–55
college, 148–51
family relationships and involvement, 153–55
options open to youngsters, 147–48
unpredictability, 140–41
vocational or technical programs, 151–52
Christmas Day, visit to relatives, 67–68
Churchill, Winston, 4
Closer Look (organization), 127–28
report, 183–199
college, 141, 147–51, 181, 182
communication, importance of, 36, 37, 77, 81, 130
community colleges, 151
community resources, 122–39
diagnostic services, 123–30

educational planning and treatment, 131–39
parent groups, 132
concentration, 20
consistency in handling (at home), 56–57
Cott, Dr. Allan, 138
cultural deprivation, 23
Cylert (medication), 137

Delacato, Carl H., 134, 135, 158
delinquency, 80
Denckla, Martha, 14
denial, 28, 31, 54
developmental lag, 6, 22, 142
Dexedrine, 137
Diagnosis and Treatment of Speech and Reading Problems (Delacato), 135
diagnostic services, 123–30
academic, 127
how to obtain, 127–28
neurological, 124
ophthalmic, 124
psychiatrist, 124–27
purpose of, 128–29
when to seek help, 129–30
diagnostic tests, 175–80
discipline at home, 57
distributive education, 104
drug therapy, 137
dyslexia, 4, 6, 17, 39, 147

Edison, Thomas, 4
educational factors, 24–25
  open classroom, 21, 91
  resource room, 92, 101
  teaching of reading, 24
  for special children, 24
Education for All Handicapped
  Children Act of 1975, 104–5
educational planning and
  treatment, 131–39
  behavior modification, 136–37
  K-P diet, 138–39
  medication, 137–38
  megavitamin therapy, 138
  optometric training, 133–34
  parent groups and, 132
  perceptual-motor programs,
    134–35
  psychotherapy, 135–36
educational therapist, 130
EEG (electroencephalogram),
  21
egocentricity, 72
Einstein, Albert, 4
electroencephalogram (EEG),
  21
emotional factors, 22–23
emotional problems, 16–17, 23,
  136
environmental factors, 23–24,
  54
  malnutrition, 23
  cultural deprivation, 23
Exceptional Parent, The, 166
expectations, 55

family reactions (to child's
  learning disability), 26–40
  acceptance of the problem,
    27–28, 32
  awareness, 26–27
  child's own feelings, 35–36,
    37
  counseling, 131
  disappointment and anxiety,
    31–32
  grandparents, 34–35
  guilt and anger, 30
  mother and father roles and
    participation, 37–40
  openness, 36–37
  parents' denial of problem as
    unimportant, 30–31
  resentment between parents,
    29–30
  sisters and brothers, 33–34
  youngsters' attitudes and, 29
family trips, preparing in
  advance, 68
Feingold, Dr. B. F., 138–39,
  156
food additives, 21, 138, 139
foreign language, 102, 103
Frostig, M., 19, 156

game playing, skill in, 73–75
Gardner, Dr. Richard, 48, 157
genetic factors, 21–22
Gesell, Dr. Arnold, 22, 62, 157
Getman, G. N., 133–34, 157

grandparents, 34, 35
guilt:
  parent's, 25, 29, 30, 31, 44,
    107
  sibling's, 33
gullibility, 71

H.E.W., 5, 169
home life, 41–60
  adolescent period, 52–53
  care and treatment of parents,
    60
  consistency in handling,
    56–57
  discipline, 57
  indulgence and
    permissiveness, 51–53
  instructions and directives,
    55–56
  organizing and scheduling,
    43–44, 58–59
  overprotection, 49–51
  rewarding honest effort
    technique, 47–48
  role-playing between parent
    and child, 48
  routines, 56
  scapegoat situation, 45–49
  special privileges, 57–58
  tension and chaos, 41–43
  time and attention, 55
  TV scheduling, 58
  youngsters' possessions, 59–60
homework, 101, 102, 107–21
  anxiety, 115, 117

book reports, 107–8, 109
"did it in school," 111
frustration with child (by
  parents), 108–9
goal of independence, 116–17
learning from a model, 109
math, 112–13
parents as helpers, 115, 116,
  117–21
pressure to be creative,
  114–15
purpose of, 109
saturation point, 118–19
science, 115
social studies, 109–10
spelling, 113–14, 115
SQ3R formula, 110–11
when to do, 118
writing down key words, 110
*How to Develop Your Child's
  Intelligence* (Getman),
  133–34
humor, misinterpretation of, 71
hyperactivity, 20, 21, 137

immaturity, 7, 22, 53, 63, 73
impulsivity, 20, 52–53, 62–65,
  116
income tax benefits, 200–5
independence, 52, 83, 116
individual differences, 22
individual educational program,
  (IEP), 94, 170–1
individualized instruction, 99

indulgence and permissiveness (at home), 51–53
Institute of Language Disability (Philadelphia), 135
instructions and directives (at home), 55–56
intelligence, learning difficulties and, 18–19
"invisible handicap," 32
IQ test, 16, 69, 144, 149
isolation, 66, 78
itinerant teacher, 95, 97

Journal of Learning Disabilities, 158
juvenile delinquency, 80

Kaiser-Permanente Medical Center (San Francisco), 138
K-P (Kaiser-Permanente) diet, 138–39
Kephart, Dr. Newell C., 134, 157, 158
Kronick, Doreen, 29, 156

language difficulties, early indications of, 9–10
language problems, 7–11, 64
Learning Center (New York), 18

learning difference, defined, 6, 29
learning disabilities:
behavioral manifestations, 7, 15–17
causation and contributing factors, 17–25
child's future and, 140–55
community resources, 122–39
definition, 5, 169
early signs and symptoms, 3–25
family reactions, 26–40
homework question, 101, 102, 107–121
language problems, 7–11, 64
life at home, 41–60
life at school, 84–106
perceptual skills, 7, 11–14, 15
social perception and, 61–83
special classes, 96–100, 105
as a term, 4, 5, 17, 32
learning disabilities specialist, 92, 95, 127
learning disability classes, 96–97
Lehtinen, Laura, 20
living disability, 143

malnutrition, 23
math homework, 112–13
maturational lag, 22
medication, 137–38
megavitamin therapy, 138

minimal brain dysfunction (MBD), 21
motivation, 18, 149
motor training programs, 134–35
movegenic theory, 134

narcissism, newborn infants, 61
neurological impairment, 21
neurologists, 5, 124, 131, 141, 143
New York Association for Brain Injured Children, 132
noises, 13
nursery school teachers, 26

One Day Everything Went Wrong (Vreeken), 42
open classroom, 21, 91
ophthalmic evaluation, 124
optometric training, 133–34, 157
organic impairment, 21
organizations, 172–74
organizing and scheduling (at home), 43–44, 58–59
Orton Society, 128
overindulgence (at home), 49–51
overprotection, 49–51

parents:
  acceptance of the problem, 27–32
  associations, 132
  rights, 105
pediatricians, 26, 27, 123, 124, 127, 142
  checklist, 125–26
perception, 7
  auditory, 13
  problems, 11
  training, 19, 133, 134
  visual, 11, 12, 16, 133
perceptual-motor programs, 19, 134–35
physicians, 3, 26, 27, 123, 124, 137, 141, 142, 143
placebo effect, 138
prematurity, 21, 62
psychiatric consultation, 124–27
psychoeducational evaluation, 131
psychological assessment, 127
psychological counseling, 43
psychologists, 5, 16, 28, 90–92, 95, 127, 143
Psychotherapeutic Approaches to the Resistant Child (Gardner), 48
psychotherapy, 135–36
Public Law 94-142 (P.L. 94-142), 104, 105

Recordings for the Blind, 166
recreation program or camp,
    76–77
Rehabilitation Act of 1963,
    149
resource room (facilities within
    a school), 92–93, 95, 97, 101
resource-room teachers, 92
responsibility, 52, 53
retention (repeating a grade),
    22, 87–90, 94
Rice, Kathy Peterson, 147
Ritalin, 137
Rockefeller, Nelson, 4
role playing, 48, 68
Rosenthal, R., 156, 166
routines, home, 43, 56
rowdiness, 80

scapegoat situation:
  at home, 45–49
  in social setting, 65
Scholastic Aptitude Tests
    (SATs), 81, 149, 150, 158
school life, learning disabilities
    and, 84–106
  bed wetting, 85
  federal legislation on, 104–6
  homework, 101, 102
  IEPs, 94, 170–71
  kindergarten experiences,
    84–85, 87
  learning disability classes,
    96–97

    mother's teaching at home,
      86–87
    motivation, 102–3
    open classroom situation, 91
    parent and teacher
      involvement, 85–86, 93–95,
      101–2
    private school, 98–100
    psychologists, 90–92, 95
    reentry into original school,
      100
    resource room, 92–93, 95, 97
    retention (repeating a grade),
      87–90
    supplementary educational
      services, 95–98
school psychologists, 90, 95
schedules, 43, 56, 58
science homework, 115
sensitivity to others, 72
sensory deficits, 19–20
siblings, 32–34, 45–47, 54, 55,
    58, 60, 71
signs and symptoms, 3–25
  categories of, 17
  H.E.W. concept and, 5
  see also causation and
    contributing factors
Skinner, B. F., 136
social maladjustments, 16, 53
social perception, interpersonal
    behavior and, 61–83
  adolescent period, 78–83
  communication between
    parents and child (rules of
    thumb), 77–78

inappropriate behavior, 72–73
newborn infants, 61–62
peer group, 62, 70–71, 78, 80
premature babies, 62
recreation program or camp,
   76–77
scapegoat situation, 65
skill in game playing, 73–75
suggestions for parents (during
   adolescent period), 81–83
summertime play, 77
social relationships, 53, 61–83
social studies homework,
   109–10
special class, 96–100, 105
special privileges at home,
   57–58
speech sounds, hearing
   imprecisely, 13
spelling homework, 113–14,
   115
Spock, Dr. Benjamin, 62, 157
SQ₃R ("skim, question, read,
   recite, review"), 110–11
Strauss, Alfred A., 20
symptoms, *see* signs and
   symptoms

*Tales of a Fourth-Grade
   Nothing* (Blume), 67
tapes, 101, 103
tax deductions, 200–205
television, 11, 14, 23, 51, 55,
   57, 58, 75, 76
scheduling, 58
time and attention (at home),
   55
typing, 103, 150, 151

universities, 181, 182
United States Department of
   Health, Education and
   Welfare (H.E.W.), 5

"wait and see" attitude,
   3–4
WISC-R (standardized IQ
   test), 16, 149
writing, 17, 24, 36, 100,
   150

About the Author

BETTY B. OSMAN is an educational therapist who has been active in the field of learning disabilities for fifteen years. She maintains a private practice in which she diagnoses and treats children with learning problems and counsels their families. She is also an adjunct professor at Manhattanville College. Mrs. Osman lectures widely throughout the New York area and gives workshops for parents and professionals. She has taught at the Bank Street College of Education and worked as a reading consultant and learning disabilities specialist for the White Plains, New York, school system.

Mrs. Osman brings to the field of educational therapy experience in social casework. She worked for several years in child welfare, placing and supervising children in foster care and adoption. In her clinical approach to teaching, she has combined the fields of education and psychology.

After receiving her B.A. from Vassar College, Mrs. Osman earned her M.A. and Ed.M. in psychology at Teachers College, Columbia University. She and her husband live in a suburb of New York City and have three children.